CU00664031

When Bridie Walker fell pregna
'no good' and written off, her lif
twenty-one it looked like 'they'
working as a stripper to support ..., ...
was already a constant companion. She had survived a stroke, a
divorce and the death of a close friend in a car accident. Not the
life that anyone dreams of. But Bridie carried on.

Over the coming years she was to build her first business.
Only to then lose it, declare bankruptcy and file for divorce
a second time all by the time she turned thirty.

Yet still Bridie carried on. She was always determined to
create the life she wanted, no matter what hand she was dealt.
When every setback merely spurred her forward, little did she
know this was creating the roadmap for her future success.

Today, Bridie is a serial entrepreneur, having spent the last
thirteen years building three successful businesses. During this
time she trained as a counsellor, CBT therapist, hypnotherapist
and a Certified Life Coach. She now helps thousands of women
do exactly what she did – create the life they truly want (but
secretly feel they don't deserve). She teaches them what she has
learned: how to let go of their past pain, how to build resilience,
how to be unstoppable.

By starting at ground zero she helps women rebuild,
restructure and redesign their lives their way. They can then
develop an Unstoppable Mindset, Unstoppable Confidence and
Unstoppable Success.

UNSTOPPABLE

HOW TO SILENCE SELF DOUBT
AND TURN UP YOUR POWER

BRIDIE WALKER

SilverWood

Published in 2021 by SilverWood Books

SilverWood Books Ltd
14 Small Street, Bristol, BS1 1DE, United Kingdom
www.silverwoodbooks.co.uk

ISBN 978-1-80042-097-7 (paperback)
ISBN 978-1-80042-098-4 (ebook)

British Library Cataloguing in Publication Data
A CIP catalogue record for this book is
available from the British Library

Page design and typesetting by SilverWood Books

To my incredible daughters, my best friends, my world.
To the quiet man who always believed in me, my Grandad.
And my dear friends, my angels in the sky.
I love you all more than words xx

Contents

Acknowledgements

A special thank you to my rockstar writing coach, Jessica Killingley. I am so very thankful I joined your course. Thank you for all your guidance and expertise – you have gone above and beyond to help me create my dream.

A huge thank you to Sophie Bradshaw for bringing my book to life in so many ways. You are simply wonderful and I cannot wait to work with you again.

To Helen, Viki, Alice and all the fabulous creative team at SilverWood – you have been so amazing throughout.

To all my incredible beta readers and dear friends Hilary,

Kirsty, Trudy, Carla, Vicky, Mandy and Tracey for giving up your time and providing so much feedback and support. I am so very grateful.

To my business coach, friend and lifeline to sanity, Kerry Chumbley. Thank you for everything you have done and continue to do for me.

To Andrea Sexton for all your support and guidance. It has been such a pleasure to get to know you and I am sure we will work together in the future.

To all of my friends and every woman I have ever worked with: thank you for inspiring me every single day. You are all beautiful warriors.

To my Mum and Stepdad for always believing in me, I love you.

To my husband for encouraging me and being one of my biggest cheerleaders throughout this journey. I love you so much.

CHAPTER 1

The Truman Show

Twenty years ago, I watched a film called *The Truman Show*. It's about an ordinary man called Truman Burbank, who, although he doesn't know it, has spent his whole life as the star of a reality TV show. From the day he was born (in front of 1.7 billion people), his life has been controlled by the show's producer. He thinks the people around him are his friends, his colleagues and his family. But they're really actors, and everything they do is part of the script. In fact, everything that happens to Truman – twenty-four hours a day, seven days a week – is out of his control. Nothing is left to chance; everything is planned.

When I first saw *The Truman Show* it broke my heart. There was something about the way Truman's life unfolds that reminded me of myself. I'd been through so much and I often found myself thinking that *surely* no one could be unlucky enough to go through this amount of pain unless it was pre-planned or intentional. It was like I could never get a break. It really felt like someone had written a script for a TV show – and they'd put me in the starring role.

I believed for so many years that positive change only happened to other people. Good things, good fortune, happiness… they were only achieved by people who had it easy, people whose parents had provided a life of financial security, people in loving relationships; the type of relationships you see in movies.

I also believed life could only be good if you were perfect and gave all of yourself to everyone. All I ever did was try to please people, and yet I ended up emotionally exhausted and burnt out. I pushed so hard against life for so long that, to be honest, I missed out on most of it. Every day was a battle, either just trying to find the energy to press on, or pushing myself so hard to please that I was on constant output, not even having the time to eat, let alone think.

I spent much of my time complaining, fighting, wishing, dreaming and hoping for a different life. And it made me angry because, even though I was trying so hard, I never got anywhere. Fed up, lost and totally worn down, I felt trapped and unsatisfied. When something went wrong for the millionth time, I'd often joke to my friends that I was having a "Truman moment". But it was no joke. I really and truly felt like Truman – that I wasn't in control of my own life, that someone somewhere was writing a script and I didn't even know what it said.

Does that sound familiar? Have you ever felt that your life is something that's happening *to* you instead of being under your control? If so, I promise you, I get it. I've been Truman. I've asked all those questions you've asked a thousand times: 'Why me?', 'What have I done to deserve this?', 'Why does everything happen to *me*?', 'How much more can I take?'

The good news is that things can change. How do I know? Because I've done it.

For me personally, reading something like this years ago would have made me laugh out loud. I would've dismissed it as total bullshit. I couldn't stand being around people who were so positive, people who, I thought, saw life through rose-tinted glasses and I hated people who tried to tell me what to do. They didn't know my life and they probably had no problems or worries of their own. That's why life was so much easier for them.

You might be thinking the same:

How can life be whatever I want it to be when I'm constantly getting shit thrown my way?

How can I ever create the life I want when I'm up to my eyes in debt? I've nothing going for me! I'm forever trying to make things better but I don't seem to be able to change the path that I'm on.

I want you to know, with every part of my being, that I get it and you're not alone. Throughout this book I'm going to share with you why I know without question that you can change your life and build it the way you want.

When you've been stuck going through life doing the same things, getting the same outcomes, yet always dreaming of a better future, it can seem as if the harder you try the further you fall.

But you don't have to be Truman. You don't have to follow the script that someone else has given you. Instead of being just a character in your life, you could be the *writer*. *In fact, you can be whoever you want to be.*

At the end of *The Truman Show*, Truman realises his life is being scripted and that he has some work to do if he wants to take back control. A quote at the end of the film really stuck in my mind. It's this:

"We accept the reality of the world with which we're presented."

Until that point, I'd accepted who I was, based on the life with which I'd been presented. I'd defined myself by what had happened to me, by my past choices, by what I believed about my future, and other people's opinion of me.

But what I came to realise, through a vast amount of study and self-development over several years, is that there are many things that contribute to how we think, feel and act, and most of it is unknown to us.

Because so much of it's below our radar, making real, lasting change is guesswork. We try to focus on the areas we believe are the problem, but we can't see the bigger picture. We're inside our own lives, and when you're inside something you can't see what's really going on outside. Just like Truman. So, we look for things to blame:

We blame the things that have happened to us.
We blame our circumstances.

We blame our finances.
We blame not having enough time.
We blame other people.

In this book I want to show you that you're not Truman. You've been in control of your life all along – you just haven't realised it yet. When you have the confidence to believe you can change things, you'll not only become more confident, more physically and mentally healthy and more successful, you'll become UNSTOPPABLE.

Seems crazy? Well, let me tell you, the idea that I didn't have to live according to the script that had been written for me changed my life. It made me realise I could be whoever I wanted to be, that I could create a different version of my life. In other words, I realised that:

Life is whatever we want it to be. We can create our own life and build anything we set our minds to.

Realising I'm unstoppable hasn't made my life a bed of roses. But it has helped me change who I think I am. It's helped me overcome the shame of teenage pregnancy and raise strong and happy daughters despite being young and broke. It's helped me recover from a life-threatening illness, get over childhood abuse and cure my anxiety and self-harm. When my business collapsed and I faced bankruptcy, it helped me to rebuild it better, stronger and more successfully.

I'm not saying all this to show you how great I am. I'm saying it because I believe YOU can be unstoppable too. In fact,

I believe anyone can use the unstoppable mindset to become the person they'd like to be.

Now, you can continue to make excuses and work on superficial crap in the hope that this will bring change to your life. OR you can take control of the script and find out what the real issues are, redesigning your life your way.

I am passionate about helping you make the changes you so desperately want and I'm going to support you all the way, but I need to be honest with you. I can't do the work for you. I know that finding motivation and making time for *you* can be a real challenge because right now you don't believe that change is possible. But it is, and if you stick with it you'll see for yourself.

To keep you on track, throughout this book you'll find short exercises that are going to help you understand yourself and your life better. Some are "Reflection Tasks". These will help you to think, and require nothing more than a few quiet moments and a piece of paper. Others are "Action Tasks". These will encourage you to make small physical changes in your life. As you complete them and start to feel differences, you'll notice your outlook altering and your belief in yourself will grow.

Your life is a journey, but you might not appreciate it because the journey seems long and hard. But when you believe you're unstoppable, you're prepared for anything that comes your way, because being unstoppable is about taking back control of your life. It's about ripping up the script you've been given and writing your own. A new story, in which you – the main character – are in charge.

Are you ready? Let's go.

CHAPTER 2

What is Unstoppable?

I'd failed at a lot of things in my life, but never so publicly. Just eighteen months after launching my dream business, I was facing bankruptcy. Just a year and a half previously, I'd spent thousands on advertising and promotion, opened with a huge launch party and held a high-profile auction to raise money for a local women's centre. But now I was £250,000 in debt, had lost my two business partners (and their friendship) and even faced losing my house.

What was I going to do?

You think I can't? Just watch me!

Starting my business was the first time I ever felt proud of myself. I first had the idea in 2006: a one-stop shop for women where they could be pampered, gain confidence and find everything they needed under one roof to help them to feel their absolute best. I wanted to include all the things I loved, all the ingredients I knew would really help change women's lives and how they felt about themselves.

It was a big, big dream, which meant a big price tag and a shitload of work, but I was all up for it. This was it. This was the thing I'd been working towards. This was going to be the turning point.

You see, until then, everyone – including me – thought my life was a write-off.

My childhood was chaotic as my parents had a very messy divorce when I was young, and my younger brother and I were caught in the crossfire. We moved from one parent to the other over eighty miles apart and barely had time to build friendships before it was time to move again.

My parents made it clear how they felt about one another and there was so much hate and anger between them that even drop-offs and pick-ups would result in screaming matches and threats. The confusion and instability meant I always tried to be "good" and do everything right. As a single mum, my mum worked several jobs to keep a roof over our heads, and I saw how exhausted she was so I adopted the role of mother to my younger brother Chris. I bossed him around as any older sister does, but deep down I loved him like he was my own. We still have an exceptional bond and our friends often say we're more like twins than ordinary siblings. I'd cook and clean, iron and organise the house, forever bleaching it from top to bottom, so my mum didn't have to do it.

The only time I ever felt good was when I was dancing. Dancing and performing was in my blood. My dad was a musician and my mum was a dance teacher and I followed in her footsteps. I lived for dancing, but it was a career I could only dream of. My responsibilities made me feel so much older than my age. In my eyes I was a grown-up, but the reality was that emotionally I was still a child.

When I was around nine, I began self-harming. I'd force my fingers down my throat to make myself sick, sometimes several times a day. It was agony, and I had no clue at the time what I was doing or why I was doing it – but I couldn't stop.

It was only years later that I understood it was due to emotional turmoil and a period of sexual abuse I'd suffered years earlier. It was just the start of my secret, internal self-destructive behaviour, a pattern that later would become dangerous and out of control.

After years of being passed between my parents like a pawn in a game of chess, in the last term of junior school my brother and I were sent to live with my dad. I'd been exposed to so much and all I craved was protection, but because needing this made me feel vulnerable and frightened, I would shut everyone out just at the moment I needed someone the most. I built a coping mechanism where I'd shield my vulnerability by acting confident and loud. But my main solution was to self-harm – in any way I could.

I began drinking, and I don't mean a few cheeky ciders here and there. I'm talking about bottles of QC sherry, cider, 20/20 – whatever I could get my hands on. I also started smoking at a young age and eventually this led to smoking draw (marijuana). I would take, sniff, eat and swallow absolutely anything to try to numb my pain, all the time hiding it deep within.

Then something happened that saved my life, although it certainly didn't seem like it would at the time.

How becoming a teenage mum saved my life

When I was twelve, I started a relationship with a boy two years older than me. I was head over heels in love. You know that first love feeling? Isn't it the most intense and incredible feeling in the world? It is – until you get your heart broken. He made me feel so special. He gave me the attention and affection that I desperately craved. I felt wanted and loved.

I was very sexually active at this young age and my relationship with sex worsened over the years. Now I recognise that this was partly due to my abuse and partly due to my need to belong and be loved, but at the time I'd no idea. It was just who I was.

I'd once again adopted the role of "mum" amongst my group of friends and I was everyone's go-to for help and advice, so it was no surprise to me when a close friend asked if I'd take her to the family planning centre as she had missed her period and was scared she might be pregnant.

When we got to the centre she was in such a state that she begged me to have a test too so she wouldn't feel like she was being judged by the nurses at the clinic. I agreed. After all, what did I have to be scared of? I wasn't the one who'd missed a period.

I went into the room and the woman was lovely and explained what I needed to do with the test. Off I went to the loo and then waited with my friend in the reception area, all the while telling her that things would be all right and not to worry. As the woman called my name, I confidently walked back into that room so my friend would see it wasn't such a big deal.

What she told me made the room spin. 'The test is positive. You're pregnant.' The next thing I recall is sitting on a chair with a woman crouched in front of me holding some water. 'Are you OK?' she asked. I couldn't think. I couldn't take it in. I had no words, no feelings. I was in complete shock.

To make matters worse, as I left the room in a trance I was met by my friend, who was beaming with joy as she presented her negative pregnancy test.

What the fuck was I going to do?

That night I couldn't sleep trying to figure out how I could get out of school the next day so I'd be able to come up with a plan on how to tell my dad. I'd never even babysat a child let alone changed a nappy, but somehow I felt a sense of calm and I knew that I wasn't going to let anyone stop me from being the best possible mum.

I vividly remember putting my hand on my stomach and making a promise to my unborn child that I was going to be the best mum ever and that nothing and no one would ever cause my baby any pain or hurt.

It was my first moment of feeling unstoppable.

Needless to say, the news didn't go down well. My dad said very little but I knew he was disappointed and my mum reacted how any mum would. She feared I was ruining my life. After all, I was only fourteen. As the news spread amongst friends and family, so did the comments:

'That's her life over.'

'She'll learn the hard way!'

'She's always been trouble.'

And on and on it went.

My relationship with my baby's dad was unsurprisingly strained and we split a few times during the pregnancy, but he was at the birth and we decided to try to make things work once she was born. I had never experienced love like I did the day I held my baby girl for the very first time. It was like nothing I'd ever known.

But over the coming weeks life became much harder. Suddenly I was told that my boyfriend wasn't allowed to sleep over at our house, even though he'd been allowed to before. I was told I couldn't stay at his house either, even though I'd been staying there most weekends since I was thirteen.

What was happening? My head was a mess. Here I was, a new mum, in an adult world, now being reprimanded and treated like a child.

When my daughter was ten weeks old I went to visit my mum, and my brother who'd left my dad's while I was pregnant.

It was the first time in our lives we'd lived separately so I was looking forward to him getting to know his niece. I knew that I'd have to contend with all the comments, especially from my gran who made it known she was ashamed of me, in her mind, I had destroyed my life and any chance of a dancing career.

I'd been with my mum for about three days when my dad called. He said I was too much trouble and having me and the baby around was too hard on his wife as they'd been trying for a baby through IVF for a number of years. In short, I was no longer welcome at his house.

So that was it. That one phone call meant I couldn't go back. I wasn't welcome. I wasn't wanted. I had been torn away from my daughters dad, my first love. Would we ever see each other again?. Would my daughter ever know her dad?. I was completely heartbroken. So dependent on the grown ups, I was stuck and I had no choice but to try to deal with the news. Once again, my life felt out of my control.

Over the coming months I felt very low. *Why was this happening to me? Why did everything always happen to me? What was the point of any of it, anyway?* If this was how things were always going to be, if I was always going to be "too much to handle" and passed along like an unwanted gift, then I was done. I couldn't take anymore.

Do you know the feeling when you've reached your limit? When you're curled up in a ball pleading with life to just stop and let you get off? The "I absolutely cannot take any more" limit? Your brain is on fire and nothing makes any sense, but it's as if a dull filter has been placed over your eyes. Everything is foggy and

23

unclear, like you're driving in the heaviest rain, your windscreen wipers fighting – and failing – to clear the way.

Well, I was there, and in all honesty, I didn't want to live anymore. But I also didn't want to leave my daughter, so I turned to the only thing I felt I could control. The only thing that gave me any release: self-harm.

From there, things continued to spiral. My mum gave up her job so I could go back to school, but once again I was thrown into a school at a crucial point when everyone had chosen their options so I had to take whatever was left. Somehow, I managed to get relatively good grades, but I battled every day, feeling like a complete failure as a new mum and worrying about how I would build a decent future for me and my daughter. I wanted so desperately to prove everyone wrong and build a career, but the whole world was against me. Or that's how it felt.

I tried to return to sixth form to do A levels but was told that college would be more suitable for someone like me. It was a Catholic school, so as a teenage mum I didn't exactly fit with their beliefs. So I enrolled in night school the following year but then there was the issue of childcare. At this time there was no nursery or crèche, so if you had a baby then it was your cross to bear. It was as if I was being punished constantly.

In the end, I had to accept that I couldn't continue my education. But even though I accepted it, the hunger for a better life never left me. It was this hunger that began my quest to start my own business.

During my early twenties I began volunteering at women's centres and charities that offered support to women who didn't have any help. By now I had two small children and had been through my first divorce, but the more my pain, the greater my desire to help women in any way I could.

I knew I wanted to create a business where I could build women's confidence so they could feel their very best. I wanted to teach them how to be the best version of themselves and help them remove the bullshit chatter that was stopping them from living their best life. I knew only one way to do this – through dance.

I approached a friend who I'd been dancing with for some time and she jumped at the idea of helping me out. She'd been teaching a pole dance class as part of a new franchise but was frustrated by the restrictions. Pole was on my list of things to offer, and she was super excited to join me. After our meeting it wasn't long before her best friend, a beauty therapist, also agreed to get involved. I worked night and day on the business plan; we'd have business meetings together and the energy was electric. This was happening. I was going to change my life and make this dream a reality.

Fast forward eighteen months. Here I was, sitting in the insolvency office, having my business scrutinised with them going over every detail of my records and accounts to ensure that its collapse wasn't my fault. My second marriage had fallen apart and now my home was also at risk. My head was in a total spin, but there was one thing I knew. *I couldn't lose my house.*

12 years earlier I'd got my own house in 1996. It was a council house on a quiet road and was perfect for me in every way. It was my pride and joy. Although I'd never had much money, I'd always done my best to make a nice home for my girls. Years after moving

in, I managed to get a mortgage, and I prided myself on owning my own home. It was my safety net, finally somewhere to call mine and I always said that no one and nothing was ever going to take it away from me.

Now I was being told that my house would be held for me for a year and if the value increased during that time I'd be at risk of losing it. In short, I didn't own it anymore.

I couldn't let this happen. I had to think of something.

So I did.

I'd built a good relationship with the manager of the pub next to my business in the centre of town. He'd let me use the upstairs function room for a show only months before so now I approached him and asked if I could use it temporarily. Fortunately, he agreed.

I distinctly remember handing over the keys to my dream business and walking two doors away to set up the poles in a pub. But I'd managed to salvage something, and it was something that I loved, and even though I'd lost my premises, I hadn't lost my customers.

I was not giving up!

I went from teaching in a luxuriously-appointed three-storey building, totally refurbished with all the mod cons and extravagant shower and changing facilities, to the upstairs of a pub just a few steps away. Of course, I was extremely grateful to the manager for allowing me to use this space free of charge but it was a small, dark, unused function room that reeked of stale beer and the carpets smelt old and sour.

Once again I felt totally beaten down by the things that kept happening to me. I was back in a mindset of self-destruction and no one recognised the downward spiral I was trying desperately not to slide down.

But I knew what I had to do, so I pulled my big girl pants up and braved it, painting on a smile and giving one hundred per cent in my classes as I always did. My students were all supportive and stayed with me the whole time. For that, I'll be eternally grateful.

After a couple of months teaching at the pub, I was approached by one of my students who'd become a good friend. She knew of a room to rent in a place around seven miles from where I was. I jumped at the chance to view it.

Now, when she said a "room to rent", what she meant was a derelict storage space within an established mixed martial arts gym. I was horrified at the task ahead. I had no money to renovate the space – just a few poles and a stereo.

I'll never forget the friends who helped me. We cleared the space and built a room within a room. Then a couple of my students' partners, who were tradesmen, took care of all the fittings and made it usable. After a lot of hard work I eventually made the move, but I couldn't help focusing on all the mistakes I'd made.

Why did I set up such a big business?
Why did I think I could make such a huge dream happen?
Who was I to think I could build a future I could be proud of?
I should have known I would just balls it up.
Why couldn't life give me a fucking break?

I was slipping. I knew I was falling back into the "Why me?" mindset, constantly criticising myself and the people around me, feeling shame and embarrassment that I had failed.

Soon enough, the old unhelpful patterns resumed – I was cutting myself again, wallowing in the past and exhausting myself to make things better. I was completely drained.

Have you ever felt like you're travelling down the motorway in the fast lane and you just can't get off? Maybe you're going so fast you feel like you can't slow down, or you're trapped in a particular lane, unable to pick up speed before another crisis hits you. So you hold yourself back and stay where it feels safe.

Or you might feel that you're stuck on a roundabout, constantly going round and round and round in circles, seeing the exits but unsure of which to take, indecision building into anxiety and fear. You want to get off but you don't even know where you're going so you don't know which way to turn.

I get it, I really do.

We all know that life is a journey, and that for a journey to be uneventful – even enjoyable – you need to be prepared. You need to plan the best route, pack everything you need, make sure you have plenty of fuel, check your water and make sure there's enough air in your tyres.

But what if the map you're looking at isn't accurate? What if it's an old version that hasn't been updated for ten, twenty, even thirty years?

When I slipped into negative thinking about my business it was like I was stepping back twenty years. I was following the script that had been given to me all those years ago – the one that said "She'll find out the hard way" and "I knew she was trouble".

I was doing my best to navigate my life, but I was reading

from an old map. If you're doing the same, then let me tell you – it's time to get a new one. The mindset you're working from is just going to keep you going down the same road. You'll choose the same paths and find the same obstacles, and then, at the end of it all, you'll end up in the same place as before. If you're reading this book, I'm guessing that isn't where you want to be.

When you get overwhelmed by life and stuck in the same patterns, the only way to start to change is to step back. You have to detach yourself from life and see it for what it really is, a sequence of decisions we make based on our experiences. As we go through this sequence, it has an emotional impact on us. If that impact is mainly negative, we'll be scarred and lost. We let the negativity mount up to the point that change feels impossible.

I've been at the point of feeling like life is impossible, hundreds of times. I've been close to giving up. I've spent so much time hating life and have missed out on huge parts of it, but I still don't regret those times. I don't regret them because through them I learnt about myself. Not only this, but I know my journey has led me to you so I can help you find an easier way. I know that it's been my calling to work with women just like you, so I can show you the clear route and the best way to get to where you really want to go.

One of my biggest buzzes is teaching beginners pole dancing at my studio in Doncaster. Why?

Because my students kick ass!

Why do they kick ass? Because despite their fear of the unknown, their worries about judgement, their anxiety, their body image issues, their low self-esteem, they *show up*.

They're willing to step outside their comfort zone, just as you'll be doing throughout this book, because they know that it's outside your comfort zone where you grow the most. It's where you can truly find *you*.

My students come despite their fears and anxiety. Some are even noticeably anxious when they arrive, but even though they have these feelings they've already made the first vital step to trying something they really want to do.

And *that* is why they are so goddamn awesome.

It's because of this first step that three months later they're able to hang upside down from a chrome pole using nothing more than their legs. It's why I'm able to see the elation on their faces that this is them. This is what they can now do.

And before you imagine these women as ultra-fit, skinny Barbie dolls with a lifetime of dance and gymnastic experience, I need to tell you that this couldn't be further from the truth. They are real women – just like you.

Now I get that you might not want to hang upside down by your legs (at least not just yet) but I'm sure that you'd love nothing more than to achieve things in your life that you never believed you could. To feel:

Confident
Strong
Empowered
Supported
Encouraged
Valued

Healthy

Successful

The list is endless.

And it's not the goal that matters, but the feeling you have when you achieve it. It's the knowledge that you're unstoppable.

I'm going to make a promise to you that no matter where you are now, YOU CAN become unstoppable, and when you do it will be the biggest buzz you've ever had.

The reason that so much magic happens in a four-week Pole Dancing Course for Beginners is because the transformation is not just physical. By pushing yourself out there and achieving what you never thought you could, you catapult yourself to a completely different dimension where you feel like you can do anything. The sky (or in the case of pole dancing, the studio ceiling) is the limit.

This is why I'm so confident that I can support you to achieve your dream life – because this is what I do. I teach women how to achieve what they never thought possible by building their confidence, trust and self-belief.

Of course there'll be resistance to the things you want to do, but that's down to a number of internal conflicts that we're going to resolve. And don't think I haven't heard it all before. In all the years I've been teaching, I've heard every single excuse in the book and my response is always the same.

'I'll never be able to reach the top' – *'Yes, you will!'*

'I'll never be able to hang upside down' – *'Yes, you will!'*

'My arms aren't strong enough' – *'Yes, they are!'*

In my role as a counsellor, I've also heard excuses like these, and again my answer is the same.

'I'll never be able to feel confident' – *'Yes, you will!'*
'I'll never have a relationship with someone who loves me' –
'Yes, you will!'
'I'll never be able to make that move or achieve that promotion'
– *'YES, YOU FUCKING WILL!'*

I know you will, because no matter how many times life has kicked me in the face I've refused to quit, not because I'm stronger or braver than anyone else, but because we all have something within us that is unstoppable. I see it when I watch women walk into a room with their head down, feeling so afraid and vulnerable and after only a couple of weeks I see the exact same women rush to the front of the studio so they can watch their progress in the full-length mirrors they'd once hidden from.

I teach everyone I work with, how to find and channel that same unstoppable force.

Listening to women share their innermost fears with me, and seeing the relationships that are formed when women feel safe and able to truly express themselves and not feel the judgement they have felt their whole lives, is incredible. I watch them push past their fears and build a new version of themselves. And when they do, holy shit, they become unstoppable.

So, are you ready to become who you've always wanted to be?
Let me show you how.

CHAPTER 3

You Matter

What do you REALLY want?

So how do you become unstoppable? Well, the first step is to get clear on what you want and who you want to be. As ever, in order to make changes, you'll need to step back and look at your life in more detail. Let's do this together.

How does that look?

Now, I'm going to take an educated guess and say that you've scored "You" pretty low. In fact, from my experience of working with thousands of women, I'd say you've scored yourself under 5.

I want to say this right now: *you* are going to be a bloody 10, OK? You might not feel it or even believe it YET, but you are a goddamn 10 and I'm going to help you become one.

There'll be lots of reasons you've scored yourself what you have and some of the reasons below might resonate with you.

Low self esteem, lack of confidence, no self worth, limiting beliefs, fear and past pain all could be contributing factors.

Remember, this is about YOU and you are unique, so take some time to think about why you've scored yourself what you have.

Does anything jump out for you?

Don't worry if it doesn't – this is only the start.

Let's take a look at things a little differently.

Reflection Task

Now I want you to put these same things in order of priority. What do you tend to put first in your life?

1. You
2. Partner
3. Career
4. Friends/Family
5. Money

Take a look at the order you've put everything in. Are "You" number 1?

I'm going to guess not, but this is why you're here. To change that. The first thing to know is:

You are number 1 - you just don't realise it.

Believe it or not, you're the most important person in your life. You might not feel it at the minute but you are, and I'm going to help you see why you need to be.

For years, I would always say my children were the most important people in my life. I'd die for my children; I'd sacrifice anything and everything for them. And I still absolutely would, but the difference is that now I recognise that by not putting myself first, I'm setting a terrible example.

I know that by putting myself first and working on myself, without question I'm giving them a better sense of how they should also live their lives. I'm also ensuring that I'm strong, happy and healthy enough to give them everything they need.

I've experienced so much loss in my life, including a number of sudden deaths of friends and family members who hadn't even made it into their thirties. Because of this, I know:

Life is not a rehearsal.

Just a few weeks before I started my business I learnt this the hard way.

During all the excitement and organising, I'd started to suffer from stomach cramps. For me, this wasn't massively unusual as I have endometriosis, which is sort of like a chewing gum that grows on your ovaries and fallopian tubes, causing pain during periods. Extreme bloating is a symptom, so for me, managing that level of pain is quite normal.

But this felt different. However, not wanting anything to get in the way of my new business, I shrugged it off as trapped wind. I spent a number of weeks chewing on indigestion remedies, and would curl up on the sofa at every given opportunity. Eventually, one of my friends and business partners became extremely concerned. I reassured her that I was fine because I didn't want a fuss. I promised (many times) that I would make an appointment to go to the doctors but I didn't find the time – or more to the point, I didn't *make* the time.

You see, I was coming from a lifetime of being told I was an attention-seeker, someone who always caused trouble. As a result, whenever I got sick, my first response had become 'It'll be nothing, don't overreact!' By following the story that I was always the one to make a fuss, coupled with a childhood where I wasn't loved or wanted, I'd learnt to always put myself last. Even now, I still don't like to make a "fuss" when I'm unwell, so even though I was in severe pain, I didn't prioritise me. It almost cost me my life.

Eventually I did go to the doctors, and when I did, I was surprised at his concern. I was told to go directly to the hospital, and when the doctor uttered those dreaded words 'Is anyone with you?', I knew I was in trouble.

The doctor gave me a sealed envelope to take to the women's hospital, but even then, on the way I stopped to collect my friend and have a coffee, still at this point completely unaware of how seriously in danger my life was.

On arrival I was taken straight to ultrasound, and after an external and internal scan I was given some shocking news. Once again, I was told that I was pregnant (*fuck!*) and it was twins (*what?*) and it was ectopic (*what did that even mean?*).

I was told to return to the ward immediately where a doctor was waiting to see me. But as I walked into the lift to return to the ward, everything started to go blurry. The next thing I knew I had collapsed. All I recall is excruciating pain and hearing alarms and seeing lots of people racing round. Then it went black.

When I eventually came round I was told that I'd been in surgery for over four hours and my mum had been called and told my situation was life-threatening. I'd been bleeding internally for a long time. I was critical, and they didn't know if I'd make it.

I realise now that being unstoppable is not the same as ignoring your own health and wellbeing. Life is not a rehearsal, and if you want to make the most of the time you have, then you need to start putting yourself first.

*

Are you with me? Good.

Let's take a look at the five main areas in your life and delve a bit deeper.

You

If you've scored yourself low – and I'm assuming you have – there'll be a number of things contributing to this. I'm going to take another educated guess that you don't see yourself as confident, you don't believe in yourself and that you often criticise yourself and your body. Am I right?

Am I also right that you place a great deal of expectation and pressure on yourself to be able to do everything? And that you find it easy to pull yourself apart? That you struggle to receive compliments?

If so, you're not alone. But have you ever asked yourself what specifically you're unhappy with? Or is your habit of criticising yourself so deeply embedded that it's just automatic?

I've found that one of the first steps to confidence is to know that YOU are your biggest influencer. Only you have the power to either keep yourself where you are or choose to move to a better place. You are the first person you speak to in the morning and the last person you speak to at night, not to mention all the hours in-between. With over 60,000 thoughts a day that's a lot of internal chatter.

For me, a lot of that internal chatter is influenced by a woman I refer to as Negative Nancy. Nancy is a loudmouth. She insists on interfering constantly. She doesn't wait for you to ask her for an opinion – she gives it anyway. She has nothing nice to say and critiques everything you do.

I've lived with Nancy inside my head all my life. But the difference is that now I know and understand her, so that when she tries to step in I tell her exactly where to go. I mean literally – I actually give her the middle finger and tell her to fuck off. I want you to learn to do the same, and throughout this book I'll be encouraging you to use your middle finger when responding to your Negative Nancy too. Believe me, eventually she'll get the message.

So ask yourself now: when you talk to yourself, are you being kind and supportive? Are you speaking to yourself like you'd talk to your best friend? If the answer is no, don't worry because we're going to change that.

First let's look at how you see your body. Do you reward your body or do you punish it? Do you choose good healthy things to put into it or are you stuck in a cycle of self-destructive behaviour? Are you body confident, or do you feel ashamed of how you look? Do you pick out your good qualities when you look in the mirror, or are you overrun with negative thoughts when you see your reflection? Do you avoid ever being naked because you cannot stand the sight of your own body? Do you look at everyone else and compare yourself unfavourably to them?

Maybe you feel like you've tried everything to feel better about yourself but nothing seems to work. Perhaps you've tried every diet plan under the sun and every exercise session to lose or gain weight but nothing you do works. Let me tell you why. When you try one diet after another and to change your body in every way you can, you're not actually solving a physical problem. What you're actually looking for is a quick fix for how you feel, something to remove the pain and the hate you feel towards yourself.

I get it. We're women and we want things yesterday, and although there's nothing wrong with wanting to make things happen quickly, a quick fix will only give temporary results. It's like going to the hairdressers. You feel great afterwards (that is, unless you do what I did once and let my friend, a trainee, cut my hair. She did a great job until her mentor told her to cut short layers into my naturally curly hair. Snip, snip later and I looked like Carol Decker from T'Pau). But although a trip to the hairdressers will make you feel good at the time and maybe for a day or two later, it soon passes. It's a quick boost and then it's gone. Whether it's through hairstyles or clothes or diets, you can change your appearance as much as you like in the hope that you'll feel confident, but I assure you, confidence is much more than how you look. It's only when you know what confidence really is and how to achieve it that you can make serious headway into changing your life. So repeat after me:

I am not my body.

Total game changer!

*

Confidence is about what you believe. You see, if you don't believe that life is ever going to be how you want it to be, then where's your motivation?

I spent years hating myself, and my body was the thing I took it out on. I was constantly changing my hairstyle and colour and altering my appearance in any way I could think of because I wanted so desperately to fix myself and fit in. I wanted to be loved and I thought this meant I had to change how I looked.

I honestly couldn't stand the sight of myself. I'd sob my heart out whenever I was naked and I hated my body so much that when I got in the bath I'd lay a towel over the front of my body so that I didn't need to look down and see myself.

The thing I loathed the most was my stretch marks – bright red, deep, horrible marks. I was so conscious of them that even with clothes on they made me feel sick, just knowing they were there. I wasted so much time hating myself. I know now that stretch marks are just a sign your skin has stretched, that it's knitted together despite being pushed to its limit. This is how I now see them, but many years ago I was repulsed by my own skin and that makes me very sad.

The main reason I hated my body was that I always strived for perfection. I believed perfection would make me more loveable, and I saw my image as the one thing in my life I could control. I'd set myself unrealistic goals and told myself that if I changed my hair, my weight, the clothes I wore, that I'd feel better about myself. I was wrong. The truth is, I never felt happy – not at any point.

While I wasted so many years pulling myself apart and

41

trying to change pretty much everything about myself, I was missing the one thing that would truly change my life.

I wasn't working from the inside.

I was focusing only on what could be seen, and I can't believe I wasted over twenty years of my life before I finally got it. So I want your commitment to yourself to start right here, today. You're going to make working on YOU a priority.

Relationships

Now that we've looked at your relationship with yourself, what about your relationship with your partner? Even if you are currently single, looking at how you behave in relationships will help you understand how past relationships have made you feel.

If you're in a relationship, maybe you think it's your relationship that is making you feel unhappy and dissatisfied. I'm well aware that some partners can be total dickheads – selfish, controlling, even abusive. Believe me, I've had my fair share of knobs in my past. But I know now that it was actually my view of myself that kept me in those relationships. I simply didn't feel I deserved any better.

Of course, not all partners are dickheads. But even with the right person, your relationship can still feel like a struggle – or even a battlefield.

We know that communication in any relationship is crucial to its success. Maybe like me, you've tried to speak to your partner numerous times about how you're feeling but whenever you do you get absolutely nowhere. So you give up and try to "make do".

I hear you. If everything is always hard work and most discussions end up in an argument then eventually you'll feel alone and invisible.

Or do you look at other people's relationships and constantly compare them to your own? Maybe they seem more romantic and romance is something you crave, or their sex life seems amazing and your partner hasn't touched you in months. Maybe you envy the way they seem more connected and in love?

It could be you see yourself as the problem. Maybe being on your own fills you with dread and you feel that you need someone in your life just to have a sense of belonging?

Whatever situation you're in, the truth is that nothing can change your relationships or your view of relationships until you are happy with YOU. Which takes us back to the first area of your life we looked at. You need to make sure YOU are the most important person in your life. And that means getting rid of that Negative Nancy chatter and believing that YOU are worth a loving, supportive relationship.

Friends and family

Good friends and/or family members can give you a great support network. But they can also have a negative influence. Have you noticed that friends and family will always offer up their opinions – with the best of intentions – on how you should live your life? This might not be in an overpowering way, but it still contributes to how you see yourself and the decisions you make. A lot of the time we turn to those around us for advice, but really the advice only causes more confusion.

It might be that a family member or friend is causing you a lot of stress and headache but you haven't the heart to say what you really want to say because you don't want to hurt anyone's feelings or look like a bitch. So you just put up with endless demands and listen to everyone else's problems as a way of avoiding your own. You may find yourself caring for a family member (perhaps because others have opted out). This can be extremely testing on your life; carrying such responsibility alone can be a great deal to manage.

If you've never had a loving and supportive family, then your view of "family" is likely to be a negative one. All my long-term partners have come from stable backgrounds with big family units, and I struggled with embracing their "rituals". I found meeting up all together – aunties, uncles, cousins – alien and uncomfortable, not because of anything they did, but because my brain couldn't process how a family could be this way.

Again, when you put yourself first and work to understand yourself, your relationships with family and friends will become healthier.

Money

It might be that your financial situation is causing you a lot of stress. Maybe you don't know where to start improving your life because you can't see a way out of debt or of being financially reliant on someone else. Even if money's not a problem, maybe the lack of fulfilment in your life is making you feel ungrateful for having a comfortable life but still feeling like shit.

Money is one of the biggest contributors to stress, BUT if you aren't happy within yourself then changing your financial situation won't help. You'll always focus on what you don't have and not on what you do.

So where's your focus when it comes to money? Do you see wealth as unattainable? Do you have enough money but still feel dissatisfied with your life?

As we work on your confidence we're going to unwrap some of these beliefs.

Career

Is it your career or lack of it that's leaving you feeling unsatisfied and fed up? Did you have ambitions that you haven't met or are you stuck still not knowing what to do with your life? What can you do to change how you feel about your current career, or lack of?

A lot of women I work with would love to have a career but worry about being too old to learn new skills and knowledge. One of my clients Angie retrained as a veterinary nurse at forty-five. It had always been a dream of hers and despite initial resistance after two months of sessions she made the leap and didn't look back. You're never too old. I went back to college to start my counselling training when I was thirty-one, because that's when I was ready. It's never too late.

If you want something badly enough you can make it happen. Here's how I know.

During my four years of study I managed to:

Run my own business.
Care for my two children as a single mum.

Finance my own study by taking on additional work.

Manage two voluntary placements (and make time to have a life).

Was it easy? Nope!

Was it worth it? Absolutely YES.

How did I do it? Well, I focused. I committed. I remained consistent. I refused to quit. But most of all, I wanted it so much that nothing was going to get in my way. That's the unstoppable mindset.

You have to want it and REALLY want it.

Your career is there for the taking if you truly believe you deserve it.

You matter

Now that we've looked at the different areas of your life, do you notice something? That's right: in ALL areas of your life, it's YOU who matters. You can wish for a better relationship, for more financial security or for a better career, you can want to mend your broken family relationships or get more friends. But none of it will ever satisfy you if you don't have a good relationship with yourself. Which is why, despite everything society tells you, and everything you naturally believe as a woman, YOU must be at the top of your list of priorities.

*

So I'm going to ask you again. Where do you come in that list now? Are you at the top?

HELL, YES.

CHAPTER 4

Every Expert was Once a Beginner

In October 2019 I received a message on my Facebook business page. It said:

Hi Bridie,

I'm interested in learning pole but I'm on the larger size and have very limited upper body strength. I was wondering if I'd be able to do it?

Best wishes, Louise.

Now, it's no exaggeration to say that almost all the enquiries

I receive start with the woman referring to her size. I'm sure this is due to the misconceptions around pole dancing and the idea that you need to be a size 10 and look like a Barbie doll in order to do it, but that couldn't be further from reality.

I addressed this with Louise immediately and put her mind at ease, explaining that pole is for "real" women: size isn't – and never will be – a factor. But after we'd chatted for a while on the phone, I found out that it wasn't just her size that was holding her back. She explained that ever since she'd had cancer ten years ago she'd been battling with panic attacks that left her with little confidence. She'd wanted to try pole for two years but had always been too scared. 'Why's that?' I asked.

'Because I'm not the typical person who does pole,' she said. 'I'm not athletic, I don't have a tiny waist and I don't have any confidence. I'm scared I won't fit in and that people will laugh at me. I could never do all that stuff.'

I smiled inside. 'Give me four weeks', I said.

The following week, Louise arrived for her first class, looking very nervous. In this class every student is a beginner and there's always a wave of nerves alongside the buzz of excitement. Everyone always stands in a line at the back, most with their heads down, and I can see them trying to make themselves invisible as they avoid any direct eye contact. Louise was no exception.

As I began to warm the students up I did what I always do – watched their body language and facial expressions as I work through the aerobic sequences. Louise was on the right-hand pole in the centre, and from the very first minute her lack of confidence stood out a mile.

I'm always aware how alien it feels when we start to work on the pole tricks. After all, holding a ten-foot piece of chrome and being shown how to spin around it isn't a natural thing to do. 'You make it look easy', they say, and I always remind them that as their instructor, I'm supposed to make it look easy, so I can show them it's possible.

Throughout that first session I noticed that Louise barely took her feet off the floor. I could see she was already beginning to feel defeated and this was confirmed when halfway through the class she came to me and said, 'I know you said I would be fine, but I don't think I'm cut out for this. I just don't think I can do it.'

I smiled. 'Of course you can't. You're just a beginner. Every expert was a beginner once.'

You see, one thing I've learnt over twelve years of teaching women to dance pole is that you have to start at the beginning. And now, as a counsellor, I know that the same is true for any work you do on yourself.

Every expert was once a beginner.

When you accept that, you realise that the only hard thing about starting something new is finding the confidence to try.

When I returned to further education at the age of thirty-one, I was so nervous. Was I too old to be returning to college? Was this something a woman of my age should be doing? What if everyone on my course was more intelligent than me, younger than me, more experienced than me? What if I couldn't do it?

I remember walking in the very first day and seeing the hall full of seventeen-year-olds and thinking, *What the hell am I doing here?* The college seemed huge – as I registered for my first day,

I was handed a plan of the campus and told where my room was, and this in itself freaked me out. I have no sense of direction and I could feel my anxiety building. I didn't want to look incompetent on my first day.

Part of me wanted to turn around, go home and give it up. But the bigger part of me had the goal in mind – becoming a counsellor for women. I knew I had to push past all the fear and doubt if I wanted to gain my qualifications, that in order to become the expert in my field I had to go through the process of being a beginner. We all do.

So why do we so often put off or even avoid this stage?

Because it's unknown territory. And when something is unknown to us, all we have is a picture in our own mind of what we assume it will be like.

Think about the first time you bought or rented a house. You'd never been a homeowner or tenant before – you were a beginner. You knew that running a house and paying bills was a big responsibility, but you didn't shy away from it. You didn't stay living at home with your parents because you were afraid of becoming a first-time homeowner or tenant. You overcame your worry about being a beginner because there was something else: the excitement of owning or renting your own property.

It's the same with learning to drive. When you start your driving lessons you know that you'll need to go through the process of being a beginner as you learn the skills required to pass your test. And you really are a beginner! You do everything

51

very consciously: hands on the wheel at ten-to-two, checking in every mirror continuously, dreading the hill starts in case you stall, shallow breathing as you make your way around. It's tough because it's new. Yet at the end of that first lesson do you rebook? Of course you do, because you're focused on the freedom you'll have when you've passed your test.

Every goal in life – from passing your driving test to owning your first home – requires you to be a beginner. Your goal now – to work on yourself and change your life – is no different. You have to follow the same process.

It's all about what you choose to focus on – what you can't yet do, or what you stand to gain when you can.

You can't achieve the life you want without going through the beginner stage. This is the stage where we learn, develop and grow. So instead of being afraid of being a beginner you should embrace it. That doesn't mean it won't make you break out in a cold sweat at times. But I'm a firm believer in feeling the fear and doing it anyway. Here's what my friend Carla said about being a beginner when she made the jump from healthcare to paramedic.

'The first time you set foot in an ambulance is scary enough if you're a patient, but it's even more so if you're a professional. Even with an intensive care background, taking that skill and experience onto the road was a completely new beginning – yes, I had the knowledge and the skills, but the practicality of it was a whole different ball game.

'I was so nervous at my first call-out. There I am, climbing through nettles and bushes to get to my patient. The fire service is cutting the roof off the car, feet away from my head. I'm in full uniform, complete with steel toecaps, and draped in a high vis and a helmet. It's fucking hot in there. And that's my patient. I'm leading this job, so I'm speaking to the fire service and managing the situation to the best of my ability. Of course, my mentor is there watching every single move I make – nothing bad is going to happen – but it still feels like being thrown in at the deep end. But that's how you learn on the road.

'It's scary as hell, but when that adrenaline kicks in, you're good. You know you've got this. I did have a moment when the tiny Carla inside my brain was screaming FUCK WHAT THE FUCK DO I DO HERE? But that's not a bad thing. It was perfectly normal for me to feel like that – I'm a beginner at this, I don't know it all. And that's OK.'

Being a beginner should be celebrated. It means you're trying something new and we all know that this is how we build on our experience and knowledge. The beginning stage of anything is an opportunity, so shift your focus to the objective and break down your progress into manageable chunks.

When I choreograph a pole routine, first of all I start with the music. I look for a song that I can connect with, a song that lets me visualise the routines I'll create to go with it. Next, I choose the style of the routine, deciding the pace and the content. I do all this planning before I even start to work on the practical elements.

There was a time when creating a routine seemed over-whelming. As with everything we do for the first time, it felt alien and unnatural, but with practice and consistency, eventually these feelings subsided and my confidence and self-belief grew. Before I knew it, I no longer felt like a beginner but someone who knows how to do this, and eventually it felt natural and normal. But what if I'd skipped that stage? I wouldn't be choreographing routines today. Because:

If you avoid being a beginner then you'll always remain one.

At the end of the hour session Louise came to me and shyly asked what she should wear the following week. I smiled. Here was a strong woman – instead of bailing out at the first obstacle, she'd trusted me and been prepared to be a beginner. She was one step closer to her goal.

Each week she came out of her shell more and more, and before long she'd managed to take one foot off the floor. On week three, when she managed her first spin backwards, she was elated.

On week four she signed on for another four weeks, and on week seven she managed to get the confidence to lift both feet off the floor. I almost cried. Louise was hooked.

Since then, Louise has gone on to join other classes and my new group, Project Sass, where I help women connect with their sexy side and feminine power, and last week she told me that she hasn't had a panic attack since the day she set foot in the studio.

To become unstoppable you have to be willing to let go of what other people think about you. That's hard enough. But, even more, you also need to be willing to let go of what you think about yourself.

You need to be willing to let go of past beliefs, old habits and the things that have been holding you back, some of which will have been hidden or ignored.

You need to be willing to forget past failings. This is about letting go of the shit that's been in your way for so long, and starting again.

And to do this I want you to see yourself as a beginner, because this is a totally fresh start.

Like any profession, you need to invest time, money, dedication and passion in order to achieve your goal. It's a given that if you want to become a doctor you need to study, be good at science, go to university and invest years into your assignments before moving on to a placement where you can progress up the ladder.

It's a necessary process, and it isn't too dissimilar to how you need to start looking at yourself and your life.

You need to get qualified in yourself.

Just like with careers, this process is not all smooth sailing. But the goal is what keeps your focus and the belief that it can and will be achieved. This is where working on yourself is especially hard, because you'll have so many mixed emotions as you go through the process. It's hard to really believe you can have the life you want and there isn't a structured time frame around it (I'm not promising that in one year you will have everything you ever dreamed of, and feel confident a hundred per cent of the time). It's because of this unknown that most of us continue to accept the way things are, despite really not wanting to.

But as you start to feel the shift as your transformation of growth and understanding begins, that's where the magic starts to work, because as well as wanting to change your life, you start to build a belief that you can.

Reflection Task

Take a few minutes to think about a time in your life when you've been a beginner. Maybe it was when you started a new job, when you got married, or became a mum for the first or even second time.

- How did it feel?
- What emotions did you experience?
- What was the outcome?
- Did things turn out alright?

I'm sure you'll have placed a lot of expectations on yourself over your lifetime and felt like you *should* know what to do and how to be. Well, now it's time to let go of that and take the pressure off yourself.

You need to get tough and start fighting against the bullshit in the right way. It won't be easy but it'll be worth it.

First, learn how to hold the pole...

Can you imagine if you walked into one of my classes and after introducing myself I flung myself upside down and said, 'OK, now you try'? I'm pretty sure that if I went with that approach my business wouldn't have lasted twelve weeks let alone twelve years, and rightfully so. As a beginner you need to learn to build the correct foundation – a strong one. This might mean knocking everything down and starting again, which can be painful, but if you truly want to change your life then, so what? Your current life isn't what you want anyway.

So, I always tell my students that before they can do anything in relation to pole they first need to learn how to hold it. This applies to everything in your life – before you can swing upside down you have to learn to hold the pole.

If you've had a messed-up childhood, been bullied at school, had wanky relationships, struggled with money and felt trapped in an unfulfilled life, your existing foundations will reflect that. And if you build on top of that foundation – on your insecurities, limiting beliefs and fear – you'll constantly be working at balancing everything to stop it from falling apart. That's no way to live your life.

I know you've probably been winging it. You've been doing your best to fathom how to manage life, and for that I applaud you. It's not the easiest thing to do. But with no clear direction you won't move past being a beginner. Because when you are *in* life you can't see things for how they really are. You're simply consumed by everything, and so the pattern never changes.

I eventually found a way to step out of my life and look at it for what it really was. I found something that allowed me to work with women in a way that was real, personal and rewarding, and I built an entire business out of it. But to get there I had to push through a lot of failings, judgements, snide comments and resistance (mainly from myself).

I have had to accept a lot of things will forever be unanswered.
I have had to learn to let go of past events.
I have had to forgive myself for my mistakes.
I have had to grow a thick skin and teach myself how to allow my vulnerability.

But most importantly, I've had to redesign myself and my life so I can be the woman I want to be and NOT who I think everyone else thinks I should be.

Just like me, there'll be things you need to accept in order to move forward to the life you really want and deserve. But there's also a lot you can change.

CHAPTER 5

You Have More Control
than you Think

Just before my nineteenth birthday, when my daughter was
five years old, I got my first home. I had no money and no
family support, so apart from the roof over our heads we didn't
have much. Nothing matched and everything I had was handed
down to me from someone else.

I'd got a small government grant which paid for my
daughter's bedroom to be decorated and kitted out and I had
enough left over to decorate the living room. Everywhere else was
floorboards and bare walls. My bedroom consisted of a bed and an
old cherrywood wardrobe with a lock and key. I had no curtains,

no carpet, no drawers, no light shade, nothing. I didn't even have a TV or an oven, just a cheap microwave and an uncomfortable sofa bed in the living room.

But I was so happy to finally have somewhere to call my home – somewhere I would always be welcome and couldn't be told to leave – that it didn't matter. But I was so broke I had to be VERY careful to make what little money I had, last.

For example, my electric supply was through a coin operated meter, and I couldn't afford a whole week's power, so I knew that I couldn't afford to make the electric last the week and I knew that, come Monday morning, there wouldn't be enough for my daughter to have breakfast and do her usual school morning routine if I didn't find a way to save an extra twelve hours somewhere in the week. Looking back, it was a pretty desperate situation, but I had to somehow make it work.

So, I devised Candle Night.

This took place every Sunday evening. I'd light candles throughout the house and tell my daughter that this was how people lived before electricity, and to always remain grateful for what we have. I made it our special time to read and play board games, and it was fun, on this one night a week, to go back to that time.

Not being able to pay for the electricity was out of my control. It felt so unfair that I couldn't provide my daughter with everything she needed, and a part of me felt worthless. I couldn't see a way that I would EVER get out of this position. But in that situation, where there seemed little I could do to change things, I found something I *could* control: my attitude. It was in my power to stay positive and even to build a fond memory for my daughter.

She often talks of how much she loved those nights, and now as an adult herself, she cannot believe the lengths I went to. But I remind her that at times of worry we have more control than we think.

I may not have had money but what I did have was:

A place that was mine.
Somewhere I could call my own.
Stability for the first time in my life.
A place to build a future for me and my daughter.

Life isn't always as you want it to be, but part of being unstoppable is knowing that everything can and will change.

It's how you look at your situation that REALLY makes the difference.

After looking at the different parts of your life in chapter 2, hopefully you're beginning to question and unpick those areas. So how can you move from feeling stuck and out of control to feeling positive and proactive? The answer is in your thoughts.

Paradigms and automatic thoughts

It's only when you learn how powerful your mind is and how to work with it instead of against it, that you begin to make changes in your life. From birth, our subconscious mind is wide open, and just like sponges we absorb everything that's shown to us.

The things we hear and the environment we're brought-up in has a major impact on how we think, feel and act as adults.

What's important to understand is that, unlike our conscious mind, our subconscious mind has no filter. It has no way of knowing what's good for us and what's bad, what's helpful and what's unhelpful. It has no clue whatsoever – it just takes everything in.

Think about a computer. If you're anything like me, you'll only know the basics of how a computer works. I can't count the number of times I've sat swearing at my laptop, losing my shit because it isn't doing what I'm asking.

But the truth is, the reason it isn't doing what I'm asking is because I'm not being clear on what I'm telling it to do. It only responds to the information I'm putting in. If that information is wrong, the computer has no way of knowing that.

This is exactly how our subconscious works.

Over the early years of our lives we absorb everything without questioning its truth. But our experiences can cause us to become stuck in a paradigm. A paradigm is a mental programme that has exclusive control over our habitual behaviour. And because almost all of our behaviour is done out of habit – in other words, it's automatic – paradigms are pretty powerful at controlling who we think we are.

For example, when you see or hear something often enough, it starts to become what you expect to see. Doctors often get stuck in paradigms because they see so many patients, most of them with common illnesses. So when they see a certain set of symptoms, they'll always choose the most common diagnosis first.

This way of thinking caused several doctors to miss a serious illness that resulted in me spending two months in a neurological ward.

I was seventeen and had been working at a local town pub when I noticed my left arm was feeling numb. I went to the GP, who declared it to be a trapped nerve, but I knew it was something else. I didn't know what, but I knew there was more to it than that.

I made another appointment to see the doctor in the following week and during that time I experienced even more loss of feeling on my left side, including one terrifying night when I woke up needing to go to the toilet and found I was completely paralysed. No matter how much I tried to concentrate on moving my legs, I couldn't.

Frozen in fear, I could do nothing but lie there. In the morning the paralysis had gone, but the fear of the previous night weighed heavily on my mind. After the second visit to the doctors they told me that it could be my sciatic nerve and arranged an outpatient appointment. But still I knew that it was something else.

This process went on for about two months until one day, after an appointment with a different GP, my mum received a call to say that I needed to go to the hospital immediately as they suspected I was having a stroke. My mum didn't tell me at the time and we went to the hospital where a neurologist from Sheffield came over to assess me. It was then that everything changed.

I was blue-lighted to Sheffield Hallamshire Hospital and within days I'd deteriorated further. It turned out that my body was responding to severe stress and my nervous system had begun to shut down. I spent two months in hospital where I had to learn to walk again and regain my motor functions. It was one of the scariest times of my life.

I understand why those doctors didn't diagnose me correctly – what was happening to me was highly unusual, let alone for a girl of my age. They were following the paradigms they were used to, not looking beyond the most obvious diagnosis. It was only when someone stepped back and looked at my symptoms objectively, they saw the bigger picture and discovered what was wrong.

In order to escape the paradigms you are used to:

You need to get out of your own head.

Being closed-off to other possibilities and assuming you already know what the problem is won't help you change your life. The automatic thoughts we inherit from our past experiences make us unable to see clearly. We don't know what we really think, act and feel like because we're stuck in the pattern of repeating what we've always done. We don't notice at the time that this is due to our subconscious programming and because we don't notice, we never think to challenge it.

Let's take driving as an example. Once you feel confident driving, you can drive from work to home with ease. In fact, we often do it without thinking. Have you ever got home from where you've been and wonder how the hell you got there because you can't consciously recall driving? This is because you're running on automatic pilot; it's something you just do without consciously thinking about it.

But what happens if you're driving along and a police car pulls in behind you? Panic! That sense of panic triggers you out

64

of your subconscious and into your conscious mind and you then start to think about what you're doing. Even though you know how to drive, you suddenly become so conscious of it that you feel your awareness shift. You check your speed every few seconds, you look in your mirrors a thousand times and do a frantic check in your mind: *Is my MOT up to date? Did I remember to tax the car? Are my tyres OK?* This happens because you are now using the conscious part of your mind to question something you've done thousands of times automatically.

Without question, it's a blessing we can rely on our subconscious to carry out so many tasks. Imagine if you didn't have this ability. Next time you're making food or having a drink, try to consciously notice every little thing you are doing. It's crazy! It just goes to show how much you do automatically.

But while being able to do things without thinking is handy for day-to-day activities, living inside your own head will never help you change your life. You won't see the wood for the trees and all you'll have is the chaos of being trapped inside your own mind. You'll always repeat the same things because of your programming.

The good news is that, by understanding where your programming comes from, you can start to change the way you think. Let's start with your energy.

Now that you've switched-up your energy, we're going to look at how to change your automatic thinking. First we need to understand what influences and experiences have created the paradigms you're currently working with. Knowledge is power and the more you understand yourself, the more power you'll have to change the things you don't like, and build up the things you do.

So, what's at the core of your central programming?

It's your belief system

Your belief system is the collection of beliefs you use as your internal compass. Like a reference guide for everything you think, feel and do. The early stages of life are by far the most crucial in establishing your belief system, because it's during this time that you're the most easily influenced. As you learn right from wrong, which behaviours are and aren't acceptable, you're also unknowingly absorbing the beliefs placed on you from others. As a child, your parents/carers, siblings, teachers, aunts/uncles, friends and grandparents all play a part in how you think and feel about yourself.

For me, growing up with both parents hating one another, constant fighting and screaming seemed completely normal, and I "took-in" that information as a reference point for how relationships are. Fast-forward a few years when I was married and had my second daughter and I was battling tirelessly with a constant, unsettling feeling that no relationship is forever. Without knowing it, I was internally preparing for the time it would go wrong, because I believed deep down that it would.

It was the internal belief from my childhood that caused me to be in a persistent fight or flight response mode in my relationship. My relationship with my parents had led me to believe that

I was unlovable.

For the majority of my adult life I believed this. I believed I was damaged goods, that no one would want me, and that the only person I could depend on was myself. Navigating my way through life with these beliefs – amongst others – was painful. I never felt good enough. I never felt worthy. Every day I felt trapped and caught up in the chaos that was my mind. I wrestled with it constantly.

Why did no one want me?
What had I done so badly?

How could I change myself to gain the love I was so desperate for?

That's when I started to use my image as a way of making myself lovable. I must have changed my hair colour and style monthly, going from real extremes: blonde to bright red, long to short, back to long again, this time with black extensions. There was a spray I'd soak my hair with. It was basically watered-down bleach you'd spray all over your hair and then dry it to make it change colour (how I managed to have any hair left I'll never know). It was non-stop.

And it wasn't just my hair. I'd adapt my clothing style to try to fit in too. From high heels and skirts to Doc Martens and jeans, to floaty dresses and sandals, I just didn't have a clue who I was because all my life was spent trying to fit in. I truly believed that if I could look right then my life would be perfect. I was so wrong. Little did I know that no matter how much effort I put into my external appearance, it would change absolutely nothing on the inside.

On one hand I knew deep down I wasn't a bad person. So why the hell did I feel like I was? My belief I was unlovable meant that in relationships I was needy, always going above and beyond to try to be the perfect girlfriend/wife. I believed that if I could just be my partner's ideal, then surely he would love me.

Wrong!

Feeling how I did meant I tried too much and when the level of effort I was putting in wasn't reciprocated I'd feel so broken that I'd go straight back to those same familiar thoughts:

Why am I not loved?
Why am I not enough?

Why is this not working when I'm trying so hard?

Let me tell you, carrying these beliefs around with you every single day can suck the life out of you. And when life then throws more shit your way you see that as validation that you are indeed unlovable and worthless. Then, my God, it becomes an absolute shitstorm.

Before I began working on myself I was totally caught up in this pattern of thinking. I'm positive you've experienced your own version of this – and your own shitstorms – too.

The problem with these beliefs is that, as you repeat them, you build on their foundations, and as you enter adult life some of them become really unhelpful. They create confusion and an unstable foundation for assessing who you really are, making it impossible to become who you want to be. Why? Because:

Your beliefs form the core of who you are.

They are the source of all your behaviours and thinking, your lack of motivation and ambition, your unhealthy relationships, your anxiety, your people-pleasing, your low self-esteem, your lack of confidence, your indecisiveness and your destructive behaviour. Those things don't come from you, but from your beliefs.

I want to show you that you can remove these negative beliefs forever.

Yep, you heard me. You have that power. You have the ability to do an internal spring clean and throw out the shit. Let's start by finding your core beliefs.

Reflection Task

I want you to think of three positive beliefs about yourself. These are qualities that you know, deep down inside, that you have.

An example might be:

I'm a great mother.
I'm a talented musician.
I'm a loyal friend.

Don't be modest. Don't hold back. I want you to tell your truth.

Now I want you to think about your limiting beliefs. These are the beliefs that have been placed on you and engrained so deeply into your personality over such a long period of time that they're what you believe about yourself. Think back to when you were younger. What did people tell you that you still believe?

An example might be:

You're lazy.
You're not academic.
You're pathetic.

Looking at these examples, what do you notice?

Firstly, you might notice that your core beliefs start with "I'm…" The reason for this is that they belong to you and only you. You own these beliefs; they make you feel good.

On the opposite side of the spectrum are your limiting beliefs. Well, those motherfuckers are not yours. They belong to someone else, and that's why they start with "You are…"

By writing your core and limiting beliefs in this way, you can start to differentiate between the two. And if you're not sure which is which, try asking yourself this: Is this what I think, or is this what I've been told?

You can undo the limiting beliefs that have been placed upon you by reprogramming them and replacing them with new ones. Just take something from your list of core beliefs. I'm not going to lie, this is no easy fix, but like I've already mentioned, nothing that comes easily is going to create lasting results.

The most important thing to remember when reprogramming your thoughts is that, while we're told numerous things about ourselves, those are not our beliefs they're someone else's beliefs about us.

Take school, for example. If in school you were told that you weren't articulate or any good with words, then as an adult you'll likely believe this is true. This might lead you to avoid doing anything where you think you'll display that weakness. You might not apply for that job, write that email, or sign up for that course.

Or maybe, as a child you were always compared to an A* sibling, and as a result you never feel that you're quite good enough. Or perhaps you were called lazy, and now you find it impossible to relax.

But those beliefs are WRONG.

Limiting beliefs only do one thing: they limit who you want to be by causing confusion and resistance. But if you take them away, you no longer have those limits. You instead believe that you can *always* learn new skills. All right, as an adult it might be a little harder to learn new things due to the distractions of life, but with practice and perseverance you can make anything happen. In other words, you're unstoppable.

*

We're going to take some time to notice how your belief system was formed through your childhood. But as you do this task I want you to remember:

You are not who others say you are, no matter how long you've been hearing it.

Reflection Task

I want you take some time now to think about those limiting beliefs, the ones you hold about yourself that haven't come from you.

I want you to take these limiting beliefs and make a counter-argument for them. I always explain this as being like a court hearing.

Imagine that you're standing up in court and a prosecution lawyer is attacking you using your limiting beliefs. Now imagine that you have a kick-ass defence lawyer, someone who has your back and is fully prepared with a counterargument for each of the charges against you.

Here's an example:

Limiting belief: you're not academic.
New belief: *I'm someone who learns best from practice. This is my preferred style of learning.*
Limiting belief: *you're pathetic.*
New belief: *I'm emotionally sensitive and have great empathy for others.*

Can you see how effective this exercise is? Every time you hear one of your limiting beliefs you can get your defence lawyer to make a shit-hot counterargument. I'd like you to take some time on this section now, but you can also keep adding to it as your self-awareness increases.

And remember: no skipping over this stuff, because what does quick and easy create?

That's right: absolutely nothing.

73

I hope that after this exercise you'll now be able to see where your beliefs have come from and how to create new ones. So now you have a choice. You can continue to live your life based on these limiting beliefs or you can choose to change them. Right now. Today.

Still with me? Good. Then you're ready for the next stage.

CHAPTER 6

You Don't Have to Follow the Script

P eople often ask me, 'So how did you end up teaching pole?'
Years ago, I'd dread this question and my answer – albeit truthful – would be mumbled.

> *'Erm, I was a lap dancer.'*
> *Silence. 'Oh…you were a stripper?'*
> *'Erm, yes.'*

You see, the term stripper would always make me feel dirty and wrong. But the truth is, becoming a lap dancer changed my life.

Finding Sky

These days, when people make me feel ashamed about being a lap dancer, I give my head a bloody good shake, because those people don't have a clue about the world I came to know and love. They don't know the strength of the incredible women I met and worked with and the reasons they had for working in clubs: to provide for their children, to make money for university, to save a deposit for a house...

For me, lap dancing was a great way to make money. As a single, divorced, twenty-two-year-old mum to two kids, it not only provided my children with financial stability, but allowed me to be there when they needed me. My hours meant that I could be there before and after school and for school holidays. For me that was priceless.

But I loved dancing for another reason. It showed a different side of myself – a side I absolutely loved.

I soon found that I could be someone else at work. Just like actresses, most pole dancers use a different name and create a character to allow them to move seamlessly from their "normal" life into a totally different world. This was super exciting for me because it meant that when I was at work, I could literally recreate myself. I wasn't damaged goods or a young divorcee. I wasn't broken or insecure.

I was Sky.

Sky was fierce, confident, driven, independent, ambitious and in control. She was a woman working to build a better future for her children and who didn't give a fuck about what anyone had to say about it. Sky wasn't struggling to make ends meet. She didn't hate her body. She wasn't battling each day with no family support. She didn't have emotional baggage and a difficult past. She was just free to be whoever she wanted to be, and that is why I loved stepping into her.

I created Sky by digging deep into the woman I wanted to be. And do you know the most amazing thing? That's the woman I've become today.

I'm confident and powerful. I gained independence, financial freedom and the ability to stand on my own two feet. By starting my own business I could provide my children with the life I wanted them to have and I did it ON MY OWN.

I'm sharing this story with you not just to tell you how recreating myself changed my life, but because I know that not everyone will be accepting or understanding of your choices. You'll get judged because people will always have their opinion and offer their advice. But they don't have to live your life. I want you to remember that as long as you do what's best for you:

You don't ever need to justify your actions.

We all have a past. We've all made decisions in our lives that were the best at the time. Having regrets will eat you up and follow you forever. So what, if Aunty Jo or your friend Helen wouldn't do what you're doing? So what? You probably wouldn't do what they're doing either. It can be hard not to get drawn into the opinions of others and I'm going to cover this more in chapter 8, but for now, know that I've got your back.

When I finished lap dancing I knew I wanted to take the best bits from my job and transfer them into a fitness class structure. I wanted women to be able to feel the release of dancing while learning awesome tricks that they never in a million years would believe they could do, because I know from personal experience – and now from seeing hundreds of women do it for themselves – that being free to become whoever you want to be gives you a confidence buzz like nothing else.

And I wanted to take it further than that. One of the things I've noticed over the years working with women is how horrendously they speak about their bodies. It breaks my heart to hear the onslaught of criticism with which women refer to the place they live. It was for this reason that, with the help of my friend Latia, we launched Project Sass in January 2021.

Project Sass

Project Sass is an online private group for women who want to build a positive connection with their bodies. We have women from all backgrounds and of all ages, shapes and sizes – real women. And just like in my pole and aerial business, all women are welcome. It's about helping them transform their lives, specifically their relationship with their bodies and their understanding of what sexy is. Sexy is an attitude that isn't based on the clothes you do or don't wear, and it isn't anything to fear, yet so many women do fear it. Sass has already been described by one of the members as a "female movement", a space where women feel free to experiment and expand their love for themselves while also creating and connecting with their alter ego. I have Sky to thank for teaching me that.

Thirteen years on from my lap dancing days, I have managed to build an exceptional business where women can come and be themselves, where they can learn the power of loving their bodies. For that hour in that class they're not a mum, or a wife, or a sister or a daughter. They're not whatever label they've been given. They are just free to be whoever they want to be. That is what I believe every woman should feel like, and what I want you to be, too:

Free to be whoever you want to be.

So, who do you want to be?

What do you want your life to look like?

Have you ever had one of those nights where you've really let your hair down and the following morning thought: *where did that come from?* Or perhaps you've got into a debate with someone about something you're particularly passionate about and, although you wouldn't normally say your viewpoint, you find yourself stepping up to speak your truth? Well, that's your alter ego – the deep part of you that is suppressed and ignored most of the time.

We all have this other version of ourselves that's hidden away and you might find she doesn't come out very often. That's because our alter ego can seem very, very different from the normal version of us. We only see her in sporadic outbursts, and sometimes these can leave us feeling embarrassed, but this is totally understandable when you realise that she's kept locked up most of the time.

*

Your alter ego is on your side. She is the exact opposite of Negative Nancy – she wants to work with you, not against you. When you're low in energy and struggling emotionally, she wants to help out, to be your best friend, and she's waiting for you to acknowledge and embrace her. She's an integral part of who you are, even if you don't realise it yet.

When you start to think of yourself as two people – the one you show to the world every day and the one that's hidden – you'll start to understand more about yourself. And, by connecting these versions together, you can create an unstoppable force, a feminine power you never knew existed.

So who is your alter ego? Well, you'll have noticed that she's the person who'll speak up for herself. She has no fear of judgement. She isn't put off by scary situations. She wears what she wants, thinks what she wants, acts like she wants and loves doing it all. She can also be extremely rebellious and this is predominantly because she is forced to hide.

To make your alter ego a part of you, you need to wake her up and give her space to be free. As you've no doubt seen, without that space she'll become rebellious and break out, maybe on nights out or in situations where your buttons are pressed. At these times she can't be contained any longer under your control, which is understandable, since most of the time you ignore her.

But what response do you think she'd give you if you gave her a voice? How would she act if you gave her a place in your life?

It's easy to stay where we know it's safe, the place that's familiar, but although this feels good because we're inside our comfort zone, staying put here actually stops you being the amazing woman you are.

*

When you learn to embrace all of you – even your alter ego – you can truly transform to be the woman you were meant to be. By embracing your alter ego you will tap into her world – her dreams, her ambitions, her goals, her outlook. You will escape the life you see with your eyes and step into a version of you that is brilliant, powerful and unbelievably free.

I understand that right now this might seem impossible. But how you will do it and in what order isn't important. I just want you to allow your mind to go wild. Think of the most incredible things you can imagine. See it all in front of you as if you are seeing into your future. And as you think about this, I want you to be aware of any Negative Nancy chatter. She will pipe up rudely and give you her dreadful input. Well, middle finger, Nancy.

(Of course, if your name is Nancy I am absolutely not referring to you.)

Creating the Ideal Version of You

You might be thinking: *where do I even begin to discover the ideal version of me when I feel so lost and stuck?*

Well, let me tell you. It was through my connection with Sky that I was able to rebuild myself, but Sky had to come from somewhere. In fact, she'd actually been a part of me all along – she was just hidden underneath all the shit.

It's the same for you. And now that you have a clearer view of the person you want to be, I promise you: she's there.

*

Yes, you'll experience internal resistance. At the moment, too much of your time is spent worrying, and being in the throes of life can feel like you're running around a human-sized hamster wheel. You never get time to stop and just focus on you. Well, NOT ANYMORE. From here on in, you're going to be putting the most important person in your life, first – YOU.

Creating *your* perfect

Let's imagine for a minute that I can offer you a complete and absolute guarantee that you can create and achieve the perfect version of you.

How exciting is that?

This is *your* perfect, not anyone else's, and because it's YOUR LIFE, you get to decide all the details. At this point in your life you might not think you have many choices or could have a life you love. But believe me, by the time we've stripped back all the layers of shit that have been added to you along the way, you'll see how much power you have.

You have this opportunity to start afresh.

So, first of all, you need to be crystal clear about what the *perfect* version of you is. This is the start of your journey, and in order to proceed, you need to know where you're heading.

The task below is going to be met with a lot of bullshit interference from Negative Nancy. You'll also feel resistance and uncertainty, because it's easier to pick fault than to believe and allow yourself to dream big. But trust me, that will change.

82

As adults, we're told to be realistic about what we can and can't have. We're moulded by society to behave and conform in a certain way. Well, I say 'screw society' because life is for living, and as it's *your* life you deserve to be living it *your* way.

So, for this task I want you to think like a child. Children have such vivid imaginations they can think up all sorts of wonderful ideas. They believe they can be whoever and whatever they want to be because their imagination isn't curbed by the need to be realistic. Children don't even know what realistic is, and that shows in their play and conversations.

So when people say, 'You need to be realistic', I say: 'Says who?'

Reflection Task

I want you to answer the following questions in as much detail as you can. The more detail you put into this the more you'll get out of it.

- Who is the perfect version of you?
- What does she do with her days?
- What type of lifestyle does she lead?
- How does she feel about herself?
- What does she dress like?
- What are her interests/hobbies?
- How does she start and end her day?

I want you to really take some time on this exercise. Grab a glass of wine or make yourself a lovely mocktail, relax in the bath or lounge in the garden. Take yourself away from your normal pace of life and really think about what being the best version of you would do for how you feel and for your life as a whole.

DO NOT CENSOR your reply.

This is about YOU and what you want, so be creative and let your imagination go wild. Nothing is too big – if it feels like it is, then you're on the right track.

Get into your vision. If you find searching for images works best for you then get searching and create a collage on your phone or laptop. There are lots of free apps that can help with this. Do whatever works for you, but remember, you need to commit to this task if you want to change your life the right way.

Give yourself plenty of time before reading on. This is a journey, not a race.

What sort of qualities did you come up with when building a picture of the perfect version of you? Perhaps you found it difficult to imagine how you'd ideally like to be. If so, I want you to have a go at the following task. It will help you to think about how others see you, how you really are and how you ideally would like to be.

Reflection Task

Draw three columns on a sheet of paper and write these headings:

1. How others see me
2. How I see myself
3. How I would ideally like to be

Once you've done this you might start to see similarities within the columns. For example, my columns might look like this:

- How others see me: *confident*
- How I see myself: low self-esteem
- How I would ideally like to be: confident

Can you see the link? Yes, that's right:

How you would like to be is often how others already see you.

So, what are you showing to others that you don't see in yourself? By unpicking this, you can start to form links of understanding. For example, if your friends see you as confident but this isn't how you really feel, is that because you're focusing your energy on the Negative Nancy chatter? Is it because your perception of who you are is overshadowed by past experiences and limiting beliefs?

If you need to, ask friends and family what they see in you and why. This can be a great way to view yourself through the eyes of those who love you. I'm sure you've heard the saying "If you could only see yourself through my eyes you would see how incredible you are". Well, it's true. When someone who loves you looks at you, they see an untarnished version, because they haven't walked in your shoes or had your life experiences.

If we use the example above about confidence, we might ask a friend why they see you as confident. They might say, 'I see you as confident because you always seem to know what to say and aren't afraid to say it.' or they might say 'I see you as caring because you always listen and take the time to understand how I am feeling' From this information you'll be able to look deeper into how you are showing up to the world compared with how you really feel.

You can also start to look at the difference between what they might see as confident and caring and begin to notice from this what you're not giving yourself credit for because you take it for granted.

When you look at the list you've written above (and you can add to it over the following days and weeks) there'll be several qualities that align and some that don't, but by writing it out in this way you can start to step back and look in more depth at how you respond. It's all about raising your self-awareness. And when you raise your awareness of yourself, you can start to clear out the things you don't want and make space for the things you do.

*

All right, so now we've started the process of creating the best version of you. It's common to feel a bit stuck at this point and find that your ideal column isn't as big as the others. Don't panic! I'm going to help you connect much deeper with your ideal.

Are you with me?

Let's do this.

Reflection Task

Let's continue with the quality of confidence. Confidence means so many different things to different people, right? So, I'd like you to think about what you see as confidence.

Every woman I work with says 'I wish I had more confidence', or 'If I had more confidence I'd feel better'. But what is this magical quality we all want so much?

It's something we look for, something we desperately want to find, as if it's hiding somewhere, just out of our grasp, lost. It isn't.

We're not born with confidence. It isn't something we have and then lose. It's attainable for anyone, but in order to get it, you first have to understand what confidence is.

If you find yourself wishing you had more confidence, I want you to answer these questions:

Specifically, what kind of confidence do you want?

- The confidence to say No?
- The confidence to start something new?
- The confidence to speak your mind, change your career, your relationship?

If you want to achieve your goals, you need to be specific. When you take the time to understand this, then, and only then, can you begin working towards it.

- What would confidence give you?
- How would a "confident you" feel?
- How would confidence improve your life?
- What does a confident woman look like to you?
- What is it that jumps out at you?
- When you see a confident woman and you think to yourself I wish I was like that, what are you referring to?

Remember: this is about what you see as confident, not anyone else.

Once you've had time to reflect, write down your list of qualities that define confidence.

When you place such a high expectation on confidence solving your life problems you're setting yourself up for a fall because confidence alone won't solve everything.

However, working on your confidence in specific areas along with working on all the other areas of your life will make a huge difference.

See this as a work in progress. It's more about understanding and working on yourself as a whole, so you know what you need to improve.

Now I want you to follow the same process, but this time look at success.

What does a successful woman look like to you?

Why do you see her as successful?

What are the qualities that demonstrate to you she's successful?

What is her lifestyle like?

What do you envisage her ideal day would consist of?

Write down as much as you can that defines a successful woman for you.

How are you doing so far? What are you noticing? Think specifically about how writing these things down is making you feel.

OK, now we're going to follow the same process once again, but this time for health.

What does a healthy woman look like to you?

How do you know she is healthy?

What evidence is there in her daily routine that she's committed to a healthy way of living?

What might she do every day to maintain a healthy lifestyle?

You see, by building a clear picture of these confident, successful and healthy women, you are in fact creating your ideal self – the woman you want to be. I know this because, from the hundreds of women I've had the pleasure of working with over the years, there are three underlying traits that each of them wants to have. Yes, you've guessed it: to be confident, successful and healthy. And let me tell you, once you have these three things nailed down, you become UNSTOPPABLE.

In doing these tasks you're going to awaken those qualities and give them a voice, because you can have all of the qualities you have written down – they are there within you, just waiting to be invited out.

*

So now you've got an idea of the perfect version of you, how are you going to get there? Well, as we know, it's all about your beliefs. So the next thing we need to do is get rid of the external stuff that's getting in your way. Or, at least, has been getting in your way until now.

CHAPTER 7

You are Not Who You've Always Been

A phrase I often hear from my clients is that they feel "trapped". I felt it too, and I learnt that feeling trapped and unable to change is often to do with where you're living your life.

For example, if you're not living your life in the present, where *are* you living it?

You must be either in the future or the past.

Recognising where you live most of the time can be a great way of taking control of your mind rather than allowing it to control you. Because once you realise where you're living, it's easier to see why you're stuck.

A couple of years ago a woman called Sarah came to me in search of answers for why she continuously turns to drink. Sarah was fifty-six and her consumption of alcohol had recently destroyed her long-term relationship and isolated her from her friends and family. Over the years she had completed several rehabilitation programmes. She described her relationship with alcohol as serious binge drinking, sometimes to the point of unconsciousness. She said she didn't know why she drank to excess when she knew the damage it was causing to her life. Until she'd started serious drinking, her life had been pretty perfect, and she couldn't find a reason for why she'd turned to drink.

When I asked her if she drank because she was trying to escape something, she replied, 'Yes. My life. I'm broken and I ruin everything.' It always breaks my heart to hear words like this and I knew, as I always do, that something was holding her back and keeping her in this vicious cycle.

After a few sessions, Sarah began to trust me and open up to both me and herself. As we discussed her life in more depth, I noticed that she brushed over an event that took place when she was sixteen. She described it as 'just one of those things', but as I dug deeper I discovered it couldn't have been further from the truth.

Sarah had been dating a boy for a few months. He was 'the love of her life' and as the relationship progressed, so did the intimacy, but one night, things went further than Sarah was comfortable with. She told her boyfriend that she wasn't ready to go all the way, but he responded angrily and blamed her for leading him on. Afraid of losing him, Sarah agreed to continue despite not wanting to. Soon after, her boyfriend ended the relationship. In Sarah's eyes she'd given consent and therefore her boyfriend hadn't done anything wrong. She believed that it was her reaction to him that caused the break-up and had spent her life blaming herself.

Over the following few months, as we spoke and Sarah shared more, she realised that this experience was the catalyst that led to her binge drinking. She'd internalised the experience and couldn't get past it, so instead she suppressed and sedated it with alcohol. She had lived forty years of her life blaming herself for the relationship ending and at the same time for not being strong enough to say 'no'.

If you listen to Sarah's words – broken and weak – then you can build an understanding of just how damaging her Negative Nancy chatter had been. Over the years she'd convinced herself that she was the issue and as a result she'd spent the majority of her life under the influence of alcohol just to try to block out the pain.

As our time together came to an end, the woman I saw seated in front of me was no longer grey and withdrawn. She was glowing and had a completely different posture and presence. She was happy and free from her past and today she's happily married and spends her time travelling and doing all the things she felt she had missed out on. I am incredibly proud of her.

Looking the wrong way

I want you to imagine that you're driving forwards but looking the other way. What do you predict will happen? I'm sure you've already guessed it. You'll crash, because you can't possibly be aware of your present while you're looking backwards at your past.

In the same way, if you're driving along trying to look around a corner a mile in front of you, what will happen? You'll be in a heightened state of urgency, and you'll probably speed up because you're in a rush to get there. As a result, you'll miss all the things that are happening right now, in your present.

In the next two chapters we're going to learn to free ourselves from both the fear of the future and the pain of the past. But first let's look at where you live most of the time.

Reflection Task

If I asked you what percentage of your time you spend in the following three areas of your life:

1. Your Past
2. Your Present
3. Your Future

What would your results look like? For example, for me, they looked like this:

1. 60%
2. 10%
3. 30%

Again, I want you to BE HONEST. You won't change your life if you're trying to kid yourself.

As you can see, I was living sixty per cent of my life in my past. I spent a lot, if not most, of my adolescence and early adult life holding on to things that made me feel rubbish. I constantly used sarcasm when making reference to my past and I would jokingly dismiss myself as "damaged goods".

But although I made fun of myself, my hidden insecurities and pain only fuelled a negative belief system. I had, without realising it, labelled myself as unlovable and unworthy. The problem was that I thought my past was my only frame of reference. I looked back and not forwards, constantly analysing the experiences I'd had. I was stuck and didn't even know it.

When you hold on to questions about your past and spend your time trying to figure out why things happened to you, it's not hard to see why you get stuck in that time.

It attaches you there.

I, for one, understand how all-consuming this can be. I know the frustration of having endured so much pain and hurt from events in your past, that you convince yourself that if you just had the answers, you could move on with your life and accept it.

It's human nature to want to resolve the past. If you feel that someone has hurt you then you naturally want to understand why.

Was it something I did?
Was it something I said?
Why did they not love me?
Why was I not enough?
Why did they do this to me?

And on and on it goes.

But what answers are you hoping for? At the start of this book I promised you honesty, so I'm going to be very honest with you now:

The answers you think you want wouldn't make the slightest bit of difference.

How often have you asked yourself these questions:

> *Why me?*
> *Why does shit always happen to me?*
> *What have I done to deserve this?*
> *Why is my life a constant battle?*

Well, here's why. Despite you being a kind, loving and caring person, life doesn't owe you anything. Life doesn't have a points system, where it keeps tabs on every good gesture you make and then rewards you with endless happiness and luck. Nope, it doesn't, and that's the reality. So, the things that happened to you in your past were not because you deserved them, or because your life is particularly shit. They just happened. But if you continue to ask these questions, seeking answers to events in your past, that dark cloud will follow you. It will find you, no matter where you are, and it won't matter how fast you try to run, it will always catch up with you. Why? Because you're living in your past.

Here's what happens when you live in your past. Eventually it sucks you up and throws you into a dark hurricane of shit. And then, just when you think it has finished, it spits you back out again, leaving you exhausted and beaten, before the process begins all over again.

Life is totally unpredictable and you never know what's going to happen next. But I do know this:

There is no future in the past.

If you cling on to questioning the past, thinking about the pain, going over and over the things that have happened, you'll stay stuck there forever. And you'll miss everything that life has to offer you *now*.

I spent over twenty years trapped in the past, replaying events from my childhood, my adolescence, my twenties all the way up to my thirties, circling back to the same questions: *Why me? What did I do to deserve all this shit?* I learnt so many lessons along the way, but none seemed to offer a solution to the question, *Why me?*

And then I asked myself this:

Why NOT me?

Try it with yourself. Why not you? It might seem harsh or insensitive, especially if you've suffered abuse, bereavement, tragedy or loss. But I want you to know that I wrote this book with you in mind. I have been you. I have sat where you are, cried the tears you so often cry, yelled into a pillow while listening to a personalised playlist of depressing songs, all the while asking, *Why can't I have the life I crave?*

*

I spent so much time unpicking and focusing on what had happened that I didn't realise it was this way of thinking that was making me feel so bad.

I wasted so much time going over and over the events that damaged me, but all I was doing was repeating the pain and feeding the damage.

I was so obsessed with getting answers from my past that I was constantly stuck there.

Specifically, I wanted answers to these questions:

Why was I never protected as a child?
Why was I never listened to as I grew up?
Why wasn't I loved by anyone, no matter how hard I tried to be the best I could?
Why did I always choose the wrong relationship?
Why did I always fuck-up?

I truly believed that if I had those answers, I could move on and start over.

But the answers to questions like these will never come, because we don't always *know* why things happen. And when shit things happen there isn't anything we can do to change it anyway, so in order to move beyond your past you've got to change the only thing you do have power to change: YOU.

I'm not going to lie: the next task is tough, so it's important that you are in a good headspace as you do it. Releasing emotion and letting go can be empowering and life-changing, but it can also be painful, so please know that you're doing this exercise to move forward, not backwards.

Reflection Task

1. What past shit do you still hold onto?
2. What are the feelings attached to those events in your life?
3. How does this impact you today?

For example, you might record your answers like this:

1. Past: my childhood abuse.
2. Feelings: I felt angry, let down, unloved, rejected, uncared for, worthless.
3. Today: in my relationship I can feel uncared for and worthless when I believe my feelings are being ignored.

In order to truly start to let go of the pain in your past you need first to recognise the emotion that's attached to that pain. After all, it's the emotion that stays with you and becomes destructive; it's the emotion that damages your self-esteem.

How you look at things is ultimately how you feel, and when you've felt strong negative emotion due to difficult – even unbearable – past events, it can be hard to alter that feeling.

As you might notice from your list, sometimes more than one past event created the same emotion and has the same impact on your present life. Over time, this repetition cements those emotions inside us and they can become grounded into our belief system. We then get stuck in these emotions and reinforce them with our current behaviour. It's no wonder we feel trapped.

So what do we have to do to get out of our fixation with the past?

We have to view the past differently.

Eventually, I realised that I couldn't change my past, but I could change the questions I was asking myself about it. I knew I had to shift my focus from what I *thought* I needed to what I *actually* needed:

1. How can I heal the young me who was abused and let down?
2. How can I make sure my voice is heard?
3. How can I learn to love myself more than anyone else ever has?
4. What can I do to choose better relationships?
5. What have I learnt from my fuck-ups?

By replacing "Why me?" with more proactive questions, I took my focus off the past and put it into the present.

Mistakes are proof that you are trying

We all make mistakes – every single one of us – but if you hold onto them they can be internally damaging.

First of all, let me remind you, you're only human. A mistake is merely a decision or an act that, on reflection, you regret. But see what happens when that regret goes on and on:

I shouldn't have done that.

I didn't mean to say that.

Why didn't I do that instead of this?

Again, letting go of the past is all about how you view it. Yes, maybe on reflection you shouldn't have done whatever you did, but you did it, and there isn't anything you can do to change it. What you can do is change how you look at it.

Living in the present allows you to truly appreciate the here and now, the little things that make life so incredible. It also allows you to stop dwelling on the past and focusing on every little thing you – or somebody else – did wrong.

In order to be present in your life you need to slow down and know that you have power over your mind – not the other way around.

Controlling your Day

Here's something I've learned:

How you start and end your day makes a huge impact on your life.

One of the most valuable changes you can make in your life right now is how you start and end your day. When you take time every morning to just sit before jumping out of bed and throwing yourself at the day, you take charge from the moment you open your eyes. Take a look at the following task. It's an Action Task, so it's something I want you to physically do.

Action Task

Each morning, instead of scrolling through social media or turning on the news, give yourself five to ten minutes just to sit and set your intentions for the day.

When I started doing this it felt so odd. I had to battle with the feeling that I was being lazy for sitting in bed an extra ten minutes. I had to resist the automatic pull to jump out of bed at a hundred miles an hour and race around. I had to be patient and allow myself time to adjust to this new way of starting my day – and you'll need to do the same.

So what does it actually mean to set your intentions for the day? Well, it depends on what you want to work on. I knew I wanted to work on my anxiety levels and therefore all my intentions were set with this in mind. My first intention was to not stress about things that might happen in my day that I couldn't control.

Allowing yourself time in the morning also gives you the opportunity to give yourself a bit of a pep talk.

'If I don't manage to do X today it's fine, I won't worry or focus on it.'

'Today I'm going to be kind to myself.'

'Today will be a good day.'

By doing this, even if something goes wrong with your day, the fact that you've taken the time to coach yourself into a calm day will mean that anything that normally triggers an anxious automatic response WILL NOT DO SO without your awareness.

That's the power of setting your intentions in the morning.

*

To make this task work, you have to remain consistent. You can't miss a day, even if you're running late, because you need to be prepared to put in the effort if you want lasting changes.

Equally as important as how you start your day is how you end it. Bedtime is usually the time when your overactive mind kicks in and worries become magnified. By deciding to change your evening routine, you can stop this cycle for good.

Action Task

Every single night, instead of going over the things you've done or said, and what you could've done differently, I want you to think of three things you are grateful for.

Write them down; say them out loud. I promise it will make such a difference.

Or you could listen to some guided meditation. There's so much available and ending your day in a relaxed and calm way will in turn have a dramatic effect on how quickly your morning routine shifts too.

You might want to think about where you want to be in your future and dismiss any fears or doubts that you can't have a future exactly how you want it.

This stuff works. I do it and I wish I'd known earlier that these two simple but extremely effective changes would create such a shift in how I go about my day-to-day life.

Out with the Old and in with the New

Your surroundings play a huge part in how you feel, and when you don't feel in a good place you put things off. 'I'll do it tomorrow' actually becomes 'I'll do it never'. But getting rid of physical crap can sometimes help us to move on from the past. Decluttering – a cupboard, your wardrobe, the attic – whatever it is, can bring a strong sense of empowerment.

Why are you holding on to pointless crap? Clothes you haven't worn for a couple of years (just in case you might wear them one day or they come back into fashion), that one kitchen cupboard or drawer that ends up full of crap and each time you open it you struggle to find what you want…

CLEAR IT OUT.

Stop waiting for things to do themselves. Stop putting off jobs that need doing in the house. Take control. It might seem silly but I promise: being assertive and getting stuff cleared out feels fucking fantastic.

The same goes for social media. Too much social media has a huge and bad impact on our lives – endless scrolling, mindless comparisons, 24-hour news…but it isn't always real, and when you spend so much time scrolling you're filling your mind with Negative Nancy thoughts.

It's time for action.

Reverse Journaling

I have always written down my feelings and experiences and I've kept many different journals and notebooks, from my early twenties right up to the present time. When I read back through them I can see the journey I've been on.

But although reading through my most traumatic times allows me to see how far I've come, I now know that holding onto all those negative things can pull me to the past for all the wrong reasons. The following task is about writing a "reverse journal".

Action Task

I want you to make a journal of all your negative and overwhelming thoughts. But instead of reading them back and dwelling on them, at the end of every day I want you to rip out the page and burn it.

There's something so empowering watching all the shit from your day burn away. By releasing it into the air, you're letting go of it there and then and making the choice not to hold onto it and bury it.

As you do this I want you to repeat five times:

I'm choosing to let go of all the negative energy from today.

I'm choosing to release it so I can be open to fresh new positive energy.

When you physically let go of something it makes space in your mind. You have a lot of important things to be focusing on - your future, your dreams, your ambitions - and you don't need to hold onto anything that doesn't fit with where you want to be.

So, make that choice and let it go.

So, how are you feeling? I know that some of this work can be emotionally challenging, so I want you to make sure you don't overdo it and exhaust yourself.

Stop for a few moments and place your hand on your heart. What is your energy right now?

Take three big breaths in and out, making sure you exhale for longer than you inhale. As a guide, you could breathe in for four counts and out for six, but this is only a guide. I want you to do what feels most natural to you.

This is an excellent grounding technique to enable you to consciously shift your energy into the present. So whenever you feel overwhelmed by events from your past, do this to help keep you on track. Breathing is something we all do, but what we don't do enough is allow ourselves the time and space to appreciate just how magnificent it is.

Ready? You're awesome. Let's continue.

CHAPTER 8

You Can't Plan for Everything

Just as it's unhealthy to spend too long thinking about your past, it's also damaging to spend too much time thinking about the future. If you're someone who does this, then my guess is that you suffer with anxiety. Instead of 'Why me?', you're always asking yourself 'What if?'.

> *What if something bad happens?*
> *What if I make the wrong decision?*
> *What if I get ill?*
> *What if something happens to someone I love?*

What if I don't consider all the "What if?"'s and I miss some-thing?

And it goes on and on and on.

Of course, you might be like me and you worry about the future "What if?"*as well* as fixating on the past. Yep, that's right, not satisfied with focusing on what had gone wrong in my past, I spent an equal amount of time worrying about the future. I would have to plan everything, precisely and in detail. Even my plan had a plan. I had to be in control and know what was going on at all times.

Here's an example.

I was so afraid of something happening to my girls that I made them have weekly fire drills. As their rooms were side by side and mine was on the opposite side of the stairs I wanted to make sure they knew that they should go into Chloe's room and immediately put down pillows at the doorway. We had no upstairs house phone and there were no mobiles at this stage so I made sure they knew how to tie sheets together so they could lower themselves out of the house safely. The girls were only tiny, but if they heard the smoke alarm they knew exactly what to do.

My daughters laugh about our regular fire drills now, and fortunately they don't see it as a bad memory, but I know that my anxiety rubbed off on them. I don't blame myself for this (I've let go of my past!), because I was doing my best to protect them and it was the only way I knew.

Of course, it's good to prepare for emergency situations, but there's a big difference between being prepared and letting anxiety control your life. Because even if you think about every detail of your life and every possible negative scenario, there'll always be things that happen out of the blue and therefore outside your control. Trying to plan for any eventuality before it happens is not only impossible – it's exhausting.

Things happen all the time that are outside our control. But here's an example of how, if we're not careful, they start to affect our beliefs.

It's Monday morning. You wake up feeling unusually refreshed. You reach for your phone... *Fuck!* Your alarm hasn't gone off, it's half an hour later than it should be – and you're late for work. You instantly feel stressed, anxious and panicked, and the more you rush to get to work on time the worse it gets. On your way across town you hit every red light, your heart rate is now through the roof and your mind is all over the place. The later it gets, the more traffic there is, until it's total gridlock everywhere.

Finally you arrive at work, but instead of relaxing in the knowledge that you've finally made it to your desk, your day goes from bad to worse. You spill coffee on your report, you forget about an important meeting, and you snap at a colleague who was just trying to help.

Now all you can think is, *MY DAY IS SO SHIT! EVERYTHING IS RUBBISH! WHY DOES THIS HAPPEN TO ME?!*

When we feel out of control, we start to panic. The fear that follows amplifies the feeling of loss of control, and before long we feel that everything is terrible. The more this happens, the more we start to accept that this is just how it is – and how it will always be.

And it's in that moment, that exact moment, that your old

friend Negative Nancy wakes up in a rage. This is how she begins her internal attack:

Why didn't you get up earlier? You're so stupid.
Why didn't you set more alarms? This is your own fault.
Why did you drive this way? You are useless at making decisions.

And on and on it goes. She turns something that was out of your control into beliefs about yourself that aren't true.

Of course, there are much worse things that can happen in life than your alarm not going off – real, life-changing situations that just jump up out of nowhere. But the process and thought patterns are the same. Something happens that's outside your control, you respond with stress and anxiety, leading to feeling overwhelmed, and you start to believe that this is how your life is. As a result, you coil up inside and lash out at everyone and anything, including yourself. You convince yourself that the only way to prevent pain is to avoid it completely. The solution? To build a wall of steel round yourself.

Building a wall

The more shit that happened in my life, the more I became emotionally shut down. At times I was completely disconnected from my own self, because I believed that I deserved the things that happened to me and that they would keep on happening. I believed they were a reflection of the type of person I was. I was convinced that by barricading myself in, by not allowing myself to need anything or anyone, I'd never be affected by anything that happened outside my control. What I didn't realise was that it was my internal belief system that was creating such an emotional war zone. And as soon as life threw me another pile of shit, it didn't take long before I was back in the same hole.

I needed to try to control something. And the one thing I could control was what I put in my body. So, I just didn't eat. I didn't look after myself. I wanted to punish myself for the bad things that were happening. I lost a lot of weight, and I was trapped in my own head, thinking, *If this is what's going to keep happening, then I'm obviously no good.*

I accepted that that was how my life was going to be – rolling along, living according to my limiting beliefs. I built a huge wall, thinking that I didn't need anyone, that no one was going to get close to me, that everything good would eventually turn bad.

The irony is that I believed at this time I was learning to be a strong, independent woman. I thought that by building a wall around me and my girls I was growing stronger. I didn't need anyone; I had all my shit together on my own.

I'm sure you've had times in your life when you've been so set on protecting yourself that without realising it, you've stopped yourself from living. Well, that was me. It's hard for me to think about how incredibly unwell I must have been. But I didn't have time to be unwell – I was busy looking after my girls, visiting my mum, and attempting (unsuccessfully) to salvage my first marriage.

My response to stress and anxiety was to "hold in" my fear. As a child I'd always been told not to cry, to pull myself together, to stop being dramatic. So whenever I felt things were too much,

I'd hear those words. Having to hold in the intense feelings of stress and anxiety meant that I was always fighting how I felt. It was far from healthy and without knowing it, I was reinforcing to myself that I was damaged goods.

My response to stress and the fear of stress was extremely damaging, but as I began working on myself, first personally and then through my counselling training, I finally saw the benefits of understanding myself. I recognised for the first time why I did the things I did and how these behaviours had formed.

Your response to traumatic events might not be as extreme as mine, but you might have created an automatic response to stress that's reinforcing your limiting beliefs.

Reflection Task

I'd like you to write down how you usually respond to stressful or traumatic events.

Do you cut yourself off, hide away and binge-watch Netflix? Maybe you reach straight for your favourite online shop and spend money? It could be you find yourself with a bottle or two of wine, or that food is your go-to when you're feeling low.

Take a few minutes to look at your automatic response to stress and, if you're able, write down why you think this is your source of comfort.

It's important to realise that the responses above are just a quick fix. And as we know, a quick fix is only temporary. Whatever you do as a way of responding to stressful situations – no matter how much it feels like it helps in the moment – it won't make you feel any better. In fact, you'll probably feel guilty that you've overspent, overeaten or drunk too much. Remember, if it comes easily, it won't last.

Managing Fear

So what's the solution to managing fear? It's safe to say we all have fears – it's a natural part of life. But it's how we control those fears that really matters. Do you face your anxieties and push past them, or do you become so consumed by them that you do nothing?

Here's a list of the most common fears the women I work with tell me about. Which do you fear the most?

Loss
Rejection
Abandonment
Judgement
Failure
Change

All of the above?

When you live in fear of loss, rejection, abandonment, judgement, failure or change, you are, without knowing it, opening up your life to be filled with all the things you don't want. These things will happen, whether you fear them or not, and worrying about them will only take you out of your present and put you into a future that hasn't even happened yet. Let's deal with each of these fears one by one.

Loss

Grief is a complex experience. It's different for everyone and comes with many varied emotions. The loss of someone we love is something we often fear, yet we cannot truly prepare for it, no matter what the circumstances.

In March 2008 my best friend died of cancer, only months after being diagnosed. I watched her deteriorate and disappear and it was one of the most painful experiences of my life. My emotions around her loss were hugely conflicted. On the one hand, I didn't want to face my life without her, but on the other, I didn't want her to suffer any more pain. I felt selfish for wanting her to stay and guilty for wanting her to go. But from her death I learnt the most beautiful lesson.

It all happened so fast. For months, doctors had been telling Vickie she had irritable bowel syndrome. But in October, the pain got so severe that her mum called an ambulance and Vickie was rushed into hospital. After a number of tests she was told she had bowel cancer. The initial prognosis was good, as the cancer was isolated and she could have an operation to remove part of her bowel. The operation was a success – but I didn't feel relieved.

Only days later I was due to attend my mum's wedding in Africa. It was the holiday of a lifetime but I didn't want to go. Vickie was adamant, though, so I went, keeping in touch by text several times a day.

I was extra protective of Vickie because her diagnosis had followed what had been a horrendous couple of years. She'd lost her job as a taxi driver, which she loved, and as a result had lost her home. She'd also been in an abusive relationship which ended badly, and she'd really started to give up on life. She'd been through such a vast amount of loss that she felt her life had no purpose.

But when she became unwell and was subsequently diagnosed with cancer all that changed. Suddenly her outlook on life switched. Her perception of "bad" altered, and she became grateful for life. In other words, she realised how much she had taken it for granted. She told me that she couldn't believe she had wasted so much of her time complaining, playing the victim of her circumstances and not taking charge.

When I got back from my mum's wedding, I heard there'd been a complication and Vickie needed more surgery. Then, at the end of February, we were told her condition was terminal and she'd be moving to a hospice. This was all too much. I couldn't think or feel or respond or do anything. I was on automatic pilot.

The following weeks were incredibly hard, but I wanted to cherish every single minute we spent together. I visited every day and just days before she died we watched our favourite film, *Thelma and Louise*. We always said we'd do "a Thelma and Louise" – run away together and go on an adventure. I remember we had to watch the film through a mirror as Vickie couldn't turn on her side. She insisted that I have a glass of wine with her (even though she never really drank) and I panicked and rang her mum from the kitchen to see if it was allowed.

As we watched the movie together for the last time, she was so weak and the cancer had truly taken hold, but even in her extremely fragile state she held my hand and raised it high in the air, looked at me and said 'I love you mate, I'll see you on the other side.'

I don't know how I managed to hold back the tears, but I did. I gave her a kiss and when her mum returned, I left for work. She never spoke a word to me after that. The following day she was too ill to see anyone and the day after that she died.

When Vickie died I remembered a line from a book I had read by Goldie Hawn. It's called *A Lotus Grows in the Mud*. She explains:

"The lotus is the most beautiful flower but it will only grow in the mud. As it reaches the light each petal opens one by one until it is in full bloom."

Vickie had been so unhappy leading up to her diagnosis and so much had gone wrong for her, but when she found out she was ill her desire for life blossomed – just like a lotus flower. My response to losing her was totally different from any other loss I'd experienced. I knew she was in so much pain and I knew there was nothing that could be done to save her, so although it happened quickly, I was in some way relieved that she hadn't had to endure months and months of knowing she was going to die.

But losing Vickie was also a big wake-up call. I realised that, while it was too late for her, it wasn't for me. I had to get a grip.

I decided to start appreciating the little things in life – the things that get lost in the bullshit of the day-to-day. The fresh air, walking the dogs, being able to walk and talk without pain or discomfort. I made a promise to myself that I was going to take action and do something I had been putting off because I was afraid of failure. That was when I enrolled in my counselling course.

If you have experienced loss you will know that it shakes your entire world. It's like a big boulder has been thrown into a lake, creating huge ripples that widen and spread. And loss can be experienced in many ways – the loss of a loved one, a pet, a relationship, a career, a home. But fearing the loss of something or someone you care for can stop you from living in the present. Vickie taught me that mud will happen in your life, but often something beautiful will grow from it. You cannot control what happens to your loved ones, and you cannot always keep them safe. But you can control what you grow from the mud life throws at you.

Rejection

As with all fears, your feelings about rejection will differ depending on what your experiences have been. Maybe in the past you allowed yourself to be open and vulnerable to a partner, friend or family member and they rejected your feelings. This can feel catastrophic. But remember:

You are not your past.

Fearing rejection because you've been rejected in the past can hold you back from speaking your truth, from sharing how you really feel in case it isn't received well and you're dismissed or not listened to.

If you fear rejection you will anticipate it and this can block a lot of progress in your life.

Let's imagine for a minute you have the opportunity to apply for your ideal job, your dream job, the one you would love to do more than anything else. You see it advertised, and instantly you feel, *Yes! This is the perfect job for me.*

*

But then something stops you. Once the excitement has subsided, you begin to sabotage yourself.

'I won't get that job because I never get anything I want.'
'There's no point trying because there will be so much competition.'
'I wish I could, but I haven't got enough experience.'

I'm sure you can relate.

You tell yourself bullshit stories that have been put in your head, not by you, but by everyone else. The self-doubt that has been worked into you over your lifetime fires-up Negative Nancy and she goes on a rampage. The result is you don't apply. (Middle finger, Nancy!)

But the bullshit stories Nancy tells you are not your beliefs. They're from your past, the old feelings from your experiences that are no longer valid because that experience has gone. Maybe you were rejected in the past, but it wasn't because of you. The truth is that if someone rejects your opinion or your feelings, it isn't a reflection of yourself – it's a reflection of them.

Abandonment

If, in your lifetime, you've experienced the feeling of being abandoned by a parent or partner, you'll undoubtedly be extremely fearful of this happening again. Why? Because it's fucking painful. Unfortunately, even one experience of abandonment feeds straight into the belief that you aren't deserving of love, that you're somehow not enough. It also creates and feeds into fear:

Fear of being left
Fear of loss
Fear of relationships
Fear that no one will ever want you
Fear that it was something you did
Fear of change
Fear of the unknown

Loss of a relationship can also bring immense disruption and emotional despair.

It can leave you with so many unanswered questions and very often make you fall back into the "Why me?" mindset.

What did I do wrong?
Why has this happened?
I'm never going to find happiness and love.

This is because the breakdown of a relationship brings all your insecurities to the front and leaves you feeling vulnerable and helpless. The only things that seem to replay are the good times and this cycle of replaying the good memories keeps you stuck in the pain and hurt. Just like a death, this kind of loss sets up a process:

Denial. *It's not, or can't have happened,* is your mind's way of protecting itself from the intensity of emotions that acceptance means you're going to experience.

Avoidance. *It's nothing to do with me.* Avoiding what is happening can be an automatic response, again to help manage your mind when it's in absolute chaos.

Anger. *Whose fault is it?* Anger and blame fuelled by the pain the loss has triggered.

Depression. *What's the point of it all?* Being pulled into darkness by overwhelming hurt and not feeling able to manage those emotions can lead to depression or depressive episodes.

Acceptance. *OK, it's happened. Now move on.* I know it's a cliché and not something you think will ever be possible, but eventually you do come to a place of acceptance.

I'm now on my third marriage, and for a long time it's been a running joke with friends that I must just like weddings. But the truth is that each time I married I did it because I believed it would change how I was treated. I thought it would change how I felt in the relationship and that marriage would give me the security I so desperately wanted. But that, of course, wasn't true.

No relationship can give you security until you feel secure in yourself.

No amount of love can make you feel loved if you do not love yourself.

My fear of abandonment made me crave the commitment of a legally-binding relationship. If you've had a difficult past, full of let-downs and disappointment, rejection and abandonment, you'll always be looking for signs that this is going to happen again. Of course, in any relationship there are fallings-out, arguments and tensions, but if you nurture a fear of being abandoned, you might:

Tell your partner to leave before they have the chance to leave you.
Exhaust yourself by smothering them with love and affection in the hope that it will prevent them from abandoning you.

122

Be so desperate to be loved that you tolerate being treated like shit because you don't feel you deserve anything better.

This last one is particularly common. I mean, some love is better than none, right?

Fuck, no.

You deserve the best and I'm going to help you understand and believe that.

So how do you change your perspective? How do you actually get a handle on the fear of being abandoned? First, you have to recognise that these responses are because of your past, not your present. Your present is not your past and the present is where you need to learn to live.

What if your current partner has hurt you, let you down and this has increased your fear of abandonment? Well, this work is going to make all the difference. It's a hard thing to accept you can't change someone else. But you *can* work on yourself.

The next thing to learn is that relationships are more about you than about the other person. When you feel good about yourself then your relationship is more likely to be good. And if you've made sure that *you* feel good and the relationship still isn't, then you'll know that the problem isn't you.

Remember, what you focus on you give power to, and fear is nothing more than a thief of energy. You can let it hold you back and keep you stuck or you can silence your fears and see them as nothing more than a challenge. When you look at fear as a challenge you'll realise that with practice any challenge can be overcome. Fear is no different.

Judgement

One thing I have learnt as a teenage mum, a lap dancer, and someone who has started her own business is that:

People will judge you no matter what.

It's easy for people to pass comments and offer advice on how you should and shouldn't lead your life, but I promise you this, leaning on other people and taking so many varying pieces of advice from friends and family will only cause confusion.

THIS IS *YOUR* LIFE!

Others will judge you no matter what you do. But so what? That's easy to say, I know, but so much harder to implement. How can you not care what other people think of you?

*

I was judged for being a teenage mum. I was looked at and labelled. But I still knew more than they thought.

When my eldest daughter was about eighteen months, she became extremely unwell. She lay on the sofa for two days, her bright blue eyes darkened and empty, refusing all food and drink. The advice from the on-call doctor was that it was a bug and I should force fluids down her until she was better.

But I knew it was something more serious than just an infection. I felt it. I also knew that I was being seen as a teenage mum who was overreacting. What did I know? After all, I was only a child myself.

Well, I knew my daughter, so I picked her up and walked her 500 yards up the road to the doctors, went straight into the surgery and demanded she be checked. When they finally examined her, they found that not only was she seriously ill with silent pneumonia, but the delay in getting her to hospital could have killed her.

Thankfully, in this instance my instinct for my daughter overrode my fear of being judged, but I hesitated at first because I felt inferior to the "grown-ups".

When you feel judged, it's like living your life under a microscope. It's hard work, but when you finally realise that you don't have to carry other people's judgements on your shoulders, you can find yourself free of fear. So, when people judge you, tell yourself this:

**They have their ideas about you –
and you have the truth.**

So, fuck what they think. Focus on you and what you think, not anyone else. And remember, you're the expert on you (or you soon will be). If you live your life restricted by everyone else's opinion you will stay exactly where you are forever – under the control of everyone else.

I'm pretty sure that isn't how you want to live your life.

Reflection Task

- What judgements do you place on yourself and on others?
- How does holding these judgments impact your life?
- Now think about ways in which you've been judged. How did it make you feel? Did it affect your decisions?
- How easy do you find it to make choices without other people's input?

Now think of a decision you have to make. Could you do it without relying on others? If you had no input or advice, what would YOU do?

Be brave and have the courage to own your decisions. So what, if you make a few mistakes? It's better than having too much input from other people. Remember, the more advice you listen to, the less you'll be able to hear your own voice.

Failure

As I said at the beginning of this book, I could never understand positive people. You know, people who live in the present, who seem unconcerned about "What if?" situations, who seem easily able to let things go. It was alien to me. I spent my time focusing on my failures and past mistakes, and the result was that I was terrified to try anything new, in case I made a mess of it.

Then I realised. By focusing on failure, I was setting myself up for it. Because by focusing on failure – either in the past or in the future – you in fact feed these thoughts of negativity. Then by rushing into panic mode you give power to the negative energy and the situation escalates. As a result, you're more likely to fail. When someone first told me:

What you focus on, you give power to.

I thought it was all bullshit. 'So, these things that keep happening to me – am I supposed to ignore them? Seriously?'

Well, yes and no. You can't ignore your present, but if you avoid doing things in your life because you fear failure, you need to change what you see as failure.

Failure is NOT a disaster. It is NOT the end.

Failure is evidence you are trying.

You can't have change or growth without it. In fact, I would go as far as to say that failure doesn't exist. If something doesn't work out, then it isn't that you've failed, it's that you've learned a lesson. And within that lesson is an opportunity for growth. But we only grow when we take action, so if you're waiting for the right time to change, the right time to move forward, it will never come. You have to do it anyway, because after all, what have you got to lose?

127

Changing how I saw failure helped me to get through the collapse of my first business. What would have happened if I'd let that one failure be my only ever business venture? I wasn't going to get it all right perfectly, first time, was I? I'd tried it one way and it didn't work, so I reassessed and tried again. Without that experience of failure, without the opportunity to re-evaluate my business idea, where would I be now?

I certainly wouldn't be the unstoppable woman I created myself to be.

Here is something I've learnt, both from myself, from the courageous women who come to my pole dancing studio and from the women I coach:

Focusing on failure stops you from being who you want to be.

It makes you so afraid to do anything that you simply stay put – never learning, never growing, never becoming that unstoppable version of you.

Reflection Task

- What does "failure" mean for you?
- What "failures" have you had in your life that you could now see differently?
- What lessons did you learn from them?
- Now I want you to think about how your fear of failure impacts your life. What have you not done because you were afraid?

What could you focus on instead that would stop you being so afraid to fail?

Around five years ago my eldest daughter was diagnosed with postnatal depression. She was and is, an outstanding mum, but having my first grandson spiralled her into extreme anxiety. She would focus on anything she felt she'd done wrong, anything she wasn't "good at", and this fed into her feelings of being an inadequate mum.

I knew I had to find a way of creating a focus for her, something to give her a more positive, well-balanced and *present* way of living. As a qualified counsellor I knew that focusing on others would help, so I suggested we set up a Facebook group to support women by offering them daily motivation.

I knew from my own struggles in life and from the lack of support available for my daughter during this hard time, that there must be thousands of women struggling alone. What I didn't realise at the time was that this Facebook group would lead to the foundation of what is today my Miss Warrior brand – a space where women can be strong and learn to wear their battle scars with pride.

And so it began. For a while I would do the morning posts and Chloe would oversee the group, and then one day she asked if she could start posting as she felt it would be a good focus for her. So she did, and over the following weeks I could see her whole life change. By focusing on the present and writing posts to help other women, she shifted her entire outlook. The result? Not only a happier and healthier daughter, but also hundreds of happy women in the Miss Warrior brand.

CHAPTER 9

You are Not Required to Set Yourself on Fire to Keep Everyone Else Warm

I had to admit it. I was addicted. *I wanted to rescue everyone.*

People-pleasing – doing everything I possibly could to help people out – had become my life's mission. It felt amazing. I was helping so many people and doing so many wonderful things to improve everyone's lives. No job was too big or too small; nothing was a problem. I wanted to be the person people called on if they needed *anything.* And of course, letting anyone down wasn't an option.

At the time I'm referring to, I was married to my first husband. I spent my time trying to please him by putting my own life and ambitions on hold so I could support his career path, which meant long periods of him travelling. I was also trying to please my children, constantly battling to not fuck-up as a mother and to give them all they wanted – quality time with me, a whole lot of after-school hobbies and endless play dates with friends. I was also trying to please my mum and my brother, who were both struggling with severe depression, by constantly visiting and making sure they were all right. I'd become a parent to them both. In short, I was putting everything into everything – except myself.

And it still wasn't enough. I needed to be doing more. Around this time one of my friends said to me, 'Bridie, if you take on any more I don't think you'll have time to go to sleep at night.' As usual, I laughed it off. After all, I was invincible, wasn't I?

When you give and give and give and give to everyone around you, what do you think is left for you? When your focus is on solving everyone else's problems and making everyone else's lives easier, what energy is left for you?

Yes, you're right: nothing.

Zero.

By doing for everyone else you're denying yourself. I understand this, because, for me, this was another steep learning curve. My desire to please everyone was so overpowering that I was constantly on high alert.

Who's going to ring me now?
Does somebody need my help?
What can I do?

I was so anxious all the time that I wouldn't even take off my coat when I got into the house in case somebody needed me and I had to go out again. I would clean for two hours, sweat pouring from me as I raced up and downstairs, entertaining my young child in the process. I would repeatedly check my phone in case I had missed any calls or messages. I was constantly on high alert, convinced that this was how I should be living my life. It was exhausting.

Here's what a standard day looked like for me:

Get kids up and take Chloe to school.

Take neighbour to the shops.

Collect boxes for friend and drop them off as she is moving house Friday (remember to arrange babysitter for Friday so I can help her move). Allow for cup of tea with friend (may take an hour).

Drop off £20 for brother and have another cup of tea.

Message friend who broke up with her boyfriend and rang in such a state last night that I didn't sleep until 2am. She needs me right now.

Take dog for a walk.

Feed youngest child.

Hoover, wash, clean house.

Pick eldest up from school and do homework.

Take eldest to kick-boxing.

Prepare tea, bath kids.

Settle kids to bed.

Clean up pots from tea.

Ring friend who split from boyfriend and stay on the phone until she's offloaded and ready to sleep.

Collapse into bed.

As I look at this now, I'm exhausted. I can feel the stress and anxiety that must have been coursing through my veins. I was 100 miles an hour from the second I woke in the morning to the minute I fell asleep at night. But at the time it felt normal. It felt like I was living my life the way it should be, helping others, putting myself last.

Do you ever stop and look at everything you're doing as if you were an outsider? If you had a friend who was living her life now the way you lived it then, what would you say to her?

When I look at this schedule now, I want to comfort that version of me. I feel sad that she lived her life that way for so long and had no idea it could be anything else. I know now that my values then were completely led by what I did for others and not what I did for myself. Maybe that's you. Maybe your life revolves around doing things for everyone else and you never have time for you. If so, you've fallen into the trap of people-pleasing. We all do it, and it's important to work out why.

Why do we spend so much of our time people-pleasing? Why do we do it to ourselves? Think about the tasks in chapter 8, where you identified your fears. If you need to, go back over them. Hopefully you can see how one or all of those fears are feeding into your desire to please. You see, when you live in fear, this fuels your need to please. Why?

In case something bad happens to them.
You don't want them to feel you've abandoned them.
You don't want them to abandon you.
You want to validate that you are a good person.

But is that how you should live your life? All that time spent on everyone else means less time to work on your own life, your dreams and your vision.

When women come to see me I often find that they are people-pleasing unconsciously. What they don't realise is that, by doing so much to please everybody else, they're telling themselves they're less important than others.

I often ask them, 'What exactly are you doing for yourself?' Sometimes they say, 'Oh, nothing. I'm just too busy. I don't have time for myself.' But more often than not, the room is filled with silence because *they don't even realise they're doing it.*

Let's see what happens when we put ourselves first. Imagine your friend asks you to pick something up for her. It feels OK to say, 'I'm really sorry but my car's going in for a service, so I don't have any transport,' doesn't it? But what about if you'd planned some valuable "you time"? Would you feel as comfortable saying no? For example, how would it feel to say, 'I can't pick that up for you today because I really need an hour's chill time before picking the kids up from school.' Could you do it? Now take a moment to imagine what it would feel like if you did. (QUIET, Nancy, middle finger for you.)

For some of us, saying 'no' is so overwhelming that we say 'yes' to make life easier. Or at least, that's what we tell ourselves. But are you really making life easier for yourself by saying yes to everyone?

Absolutely not.

You end up trying to do forty-eight hours' worth of jobs in a twenty-four-hour day, and, as a result, you feel under pressure, stressed out, anxious and resentful of all those people who seem to live at a slower pace.

Without realising it, by constantly trying to please everyone and never saying no, I was just looking to be valued.

I wanted to be needed.

I wanted to be that person who would never let anybody down, because I had been let down so much. I never wanted anybody to feel like I had, alone, helpless, not enough.

I want you to sit with that feeling for a moment, and I want you to ask yourself this:

How valued do you think you are? Just you?

What's your motivation to help everyone? Is your motivation to help others greater than the motivation to help yourself? If it is, why is that?

I used to people-please to the point where I would go without food. I would take out doorstep loans with sky-high interest rates because friends were struggling financially and I couldn't handle seeing them go without. At the time I thought I was being an amazing friend, that it was just money, and that it didn't matter that I could barely cover my own bills – as long as they were OK.

But I was WRONG.

There's a big difference between supporting a friend and trying to rescue them. If you spend your life trying to rescue everyone, how will they ever learn for themselves? If I stood in my class and showed my students a move and then went round physically manoeuvring them into position, how would they ever improve or gain their own confidence?

Saying 'no' isn't a bad thing – for you or for your friends and family. If you take a look at your limiting beliefs then it's likely you'll see that they feed into this people-pleasing behaviour. Of course it's good to help – to be a good friend, a good wife, a good partner, a good mum, a good daughter. It's good to be a giver and generosity is a great quality to have. But not if you're giving so much of yourself that you have nothing left for you. As I've said already and will say again:

YOU MATTER.

By over-giving to others, you're subconsciously telling yourself that what *you* need isn't important. And this reinforces the limiting belief that your only role is to give. Of course, you validate your giving by telling yourself that if you give enough then eventually someone will love you back, that if you give, give, give and keep saying 'Yes, yes, yes', then when you need someone, they'll be there. By wanting to rescue everybody and not let them down, you're ultimately trying to avoid rejection and abandonment.

Well, know this: the belief that you're unlovable, unworthy and not "enough" is *not your belief.*

When you learn that you can be loved, valued and appreciated just for being you, you'll have the confidence to look after yourself without feeling guilty. You'll also learn to:

SAY NO.

Remember: becoming unstoppable is all about creating the best life for *you*. So pick your head out of your hands and let's get to work on putting yourself first.

I'm going to be honest. When I first started to say no, I hated it. I was so uncomfortable that I can't even find the words to explain fully to you how I felt. But I'm pretty sure you can relate. I would work myself up into a frenzy and come up with reams of justifications to make myself feel better:

> *'I would, but something really important is happening.'*
> *'I mean, it's not that you're not important…it's just this is pre-planned. Otherwise I would…'*

On and on I'd go, through endless apologies because I felt so bad. Of course, I had no need to apologise. But when you've always been a "Yes" person you have to train yourself to say 'No'. Not only this, but you have to train your friends and family to hear it. That's because by always saying yes, you've created a level of expectation that you'll be there no matter what. At first, saying no might be met with some shocked and confused faces, but don't be alarmed. And whatever you do, DO NOT change your mind and say yes!

There are givers and takers in this world and if you have takers in your life then you're better off without them anyway. Saying no once in a while is a sure way to filter them out without them even noticing. Of course, by "takers" I don't mean people who sometimes lean on you for support. I mean people who expect you to do, bring, fetch and carry for them, who act like you've said yes before you've even given an answer:

'You don't mind, do you? You'll do that for me. You're such a good friend.'

Well, it's got to stop.

Just like with everything else, the more you practise, the easier it will be. Remember: you're a beginner! So don't be too hard on yourself. Your real friends know that you're a caring person. They value you for who you are and they don't need or want you to be doing everything for them all the time. If they expect you to be their rescuer, then you're better off stepping away from them.

This is your life and you need to live it for you.

And if you're still not sure how to say no without giving lots of reasons and justifying your decision, here's an example:

'No. I'm really sorry but I can't tonight.'

Just sit with that for a moment – the thought of saying no.

If you can, you could share how you feel, honestly and openly, about saying no:

'I really hate saying no. I just really need some downtime and time to relax.'

And breathe.

That's all it takes; a couple of sentences.

Asking for Help

The next step in putting yourself first is to accept that you'll sometimes need help yourself. Many of the women I work with don't say how they really feel because of the fear of being vulnerable or not listened to. Instead, they persist with the belief that in order to get anything done they need to do it themselves. So, they battle on, never asking for what they want.

I get it. But this goes back to past experiences, your limiting beliefs, and your desire to people-please. So how can you give up the need to be in control? When you've experienced immense hurt, pain, rejection, abandonment or even abuse you'll have felt completely out of control. Attached to the feeling of not being in control are a whole bundle of negative and painful emotions. Naturally, you believe you're doing all you can by staying in control of everything and avoiding situations where you'll once again be exposed to such difficult feelings. Why wouldn't you do this? It's become part of your survival. BUT that doesn't mean that this is the right way to be. Feeling the need to always be in control is not only exhausting, it can make you resent the people who could take some of the pressure off you, even though you haven't asked them to.

It's not always better to do things yourself.

Of course, if this is how you have always been, it won't be an easy task to simply undo it all and rebuild your beliefs, but you can change it by starting small.

Action Task

Think of all the things you struggle to do by yourself.

What thing or things could you delegate?

How could you organise your schedule to be more efficient?

Choose something you feel a little uncomfortable with – it doesn't have to be anything major – and decide to let go of the reins completely.

Your partner might not wash and put away the dishes as you would like, but does that mean they're doing something wrong? Be open and honest, saying, "This is really hard for me to do, but I'm feeling worn down and I'd like your help with..."

Try it today.

When asking for help (or not), it's easy to become a martyr. So remember:

Communication is key.

If everyone in your life sees you as constantly busy and always doing everything yourself, then chances are they'll assume you're happy living that way. Is how you feel on the inside being communicated in the right way on the outside?

I used to get so frustrated with everyone in my life because while I was always so stressed and busy, all they seemed to be capable of was adding to my to-do list. They didn't seem to care how it impacted me. This was not the case, of course – it was me. Externally, I was showing everyone that I was fine, but then several times a week I was crying in the bath wondering why I had to do everything myself. You can see how conflicting it is, so for someone on the outside it can be even more confusing.

When you want help but fear relinquishing control, you don't communicate what you actually want and it becomes a vicious circle.

So please take some time to reflect on this section and look at what you're communicating. All it takes is honesty, and you'll start to live your life for YOU.

CHAPTER 10

Becoming Unstoppable

It's time to redesign your life, your way!

This is where the magic really starts.

When you truly let go of all the stuff you've been carrying for so long, the fears you have about the future and the limiting beliefs you've been working from most of your life, you create your own blank canvas.

From right now, *you* are in complete control of your future.

The past will always remain where it should be – in the past – and, although at times there'll be testing points where things crop up, you're now more aware of them and more prepared to manage them in the right way.

Your future will also remain unknown – as it's always been. And that's all right, because you're no longer living your life in fear of loss, judgement, failure or rejection. You've unpicked the things that have been standing in your way, things that have been absorbing your energy and attention, and now it's time to step forwards into your power and your unique awesomeness.

Remember, you weren't given a rule book at the start of life, there were no guidelines to follow, no secret formula taught in school. You were left to try to figure stuff out for yourself. Well, you're not alone. I want you to work with me and thousands of other women to help you build that belief in yourself. I want you to know that this journey is going to be worth it. You have to stick to it. You have to want change more than you want anything else. And for that, you have to be willing to cut through the bullshit, let go of the excuses, and be willing to commit to *you*.

The next step is that you've got to believe. You must believe that you are the ultimate woman, the woman who has everything, the woman who isn't held back by the opinions of others, the woman who isn't defined by her past, the woman who refuses to let fear rule her life.

YOU ARE that woman.

*

All you need to do is believe that you are, act like you are and give power to the thoughts that are going to help bring her to life. You can achieve the absolute ideal version of you simply by believing that you can. Your life isn't about sitting on the sidelines, observing, hoping and wishing for change. It's about seeing how you want your life to be and committing to it.

You can have it all.

But you need to start believing it and living each day as if you already are that woman.

When I became a mum at fourteen, I didn't know how I was ever going to create the life I dreamed of. I allowed frustration, pain, anger, resentment and a million other negative thoughts and feelings to rule my life, and because of that I battled through exhaustion, stress and overwhelm – a state of being beset by intense emotion that is difficult to manage. But I managed to turn my life around because I always believed deep down that I was destined for better things, and that belief has led me to where I am today: a confident woman who isn't afraid to be who I want to be. A successful woman with two incredible businesses. A healthy woman who no longer latches onto destructive behaviour and harmful habits.

If I can do it, I know that you can, and I can't wait for you to step into your power and say a big 'fuck you' to your pain.

*

To do this, I want you to remember that *you* are special. I want you to treat yourself as the most precious thing on earth, because you are. That means taking time to continuously work on yourself – after all, you deserve the best and you set the standards. It means surrounding yourself with people who inspire and motivate you, and doing at least one thing every day to make yourself feel good about YOU.

It also means making a promise to yourself. As you come to the end of this book I want to say how fucking proud I am of you. You're amazing, and I want to make sure that the words in this book are not lost after you finish it. So I want you to make a promise to yourself that this is just the beginning. Everything you've reflected on and done as you've read this book will create a new foundation for you, a kick-ass base on which to rebuild your life your way.

I want you to write your promise in a letter, a love letter to you from you. I want you to promise yourself that, no matter what, from now on you're going to put yourself first. That you're going to allow for slip-ups and be kind to yourself when they happen – after all, this is life, and change only comes when you're persistent. I want you to promise yourself that you won't give in to Negative Nancy's bullshit and that you'll address any limiting beliefs with a counterargument.

I want you to promise yourself that even in dark days you won't turn against yourself but instead will nurture and comfort yourself until you're ready to get up again.

*

I want you to promise yourself that you'll never give up.

You are an amazing woman and I want to thank you from the bottom of my heart for choosing to come on this journey with me. You have no idea what it means to me.

Now go – this is the start of the rest of your life.

If You Enjoyed This Book...

Come join me and discover all the ways you can reconnect, grow and become truly Unstoppable.

Join my FREE female empowerment Facebook Group Miss Warrior:
https://www.subscribepage.com/miss_warrior

Join my 6-week course Unstoppable and take your confidence to the next level:
https://bridie-walker.com/unstoppable/

1:1 coaching packages:
https://bridie-walker.com/one-to-one/

With Love

Bridie ♥ xx

Lightning Source UK Ltd.
Milton Keynes UK
UKHW040701010622
403831UK00001B/31